The Science of Daily Self-Discipline and No Excuses Lifestyle

Practical Exercises to Strengthen Your Willpower and Overcoming Procrastination for Success in Life by Creating Atomic Habits

Stephen Edgar Eric

Contents

I Will Teach You to Master Self-Discipline

Learn the 12 Rules to Take Back Control and Ownership of Your Life. Used by Navy SEALs, Champions, and Athletes. See the Effects in 3 Days or Less

Chapter 1:
Building Long-Term Success

How can I do to become more successful? How can I be successful in all areas of my life, be it personal or professional? These are the questions that go around in most people's lives, always thinking of how they can become better in whatever they have set up their minds to. A lot of literature has been written concerning this subject over a very long time, but none of them have gone into details to give an elaborate formula that can make you become a man or woman of your dreams. That is why we have dedicated this first chapter of this book to enlighten you what foundation for success is and how to practice them in your life. In this chapter, we shall show you why self-discipline, overcoming temptation and procrastination, developing willpower and management of your time are the foundation for success.

Professional or personal development is solely dependent on you, and so you will need to be careful about how you carry yourself along if you are to achieve anything substantial in your life. You should note that no personal success can be attained or even a goal realized without working on your personal traits. I will encourage you to read on so that you may be enlightened.

Self-Discipline as A Foundation for Success

Self-discipline plays a significant role in personal success and achievements. In fact, no success can be realized in any area of your life without self-discipline. This is the single most essential personal attribute that is required for you to have any kind of personal excellence, career excellence, excellence in athletics and have an overall outstanding performance.

What Is Self-Discipline?

Self-discipline is known as the ability of an individual to control his or her impulses, desires, emotions, and behavior. Self-discipline can also be defined as the ability of a person to forego immediate pleasure and instant gratification so that he/she can gain satisfaction and fulfillment in the long-term. This comes from achieving higher and more important goals. When you possess self-discipline, you can make decisions, ensure actions and carry out your plan game despite the many obstacles, difficulties, and discomfort that you might face on the way.

However, living a disciplined life does not entail that you need to live a restrictive or limiting life. It does not also mean that you give up everything that gives you enjoyment, relaxation, and satisfaction. Self-discipline entails being able to focus both your mind and energies towards achieving specific set goals and stay put until they are achieved. It also gives you an opportunity to cultivate a mindset that will allow you to be ruled by choices that you have made deliberately as opposed to your emotions, bad habits or influence from other people. Being self-disciplined will enable you to achieve your goals in the set timeframe and have a life that is orderly and satisfying.

How Do You Develop Self-Discipline?

If you are dreaming of creating self-discipline like the one you see other people possess, all is not lost. Having that discipline is critical in the success of your career. It is paramount that you learn the tricks that will help you become more self-disciplined. Below we shall guide you on how you can develop your self-discipline and exceed the level that you are in currently:

Begin with Small Steps

No single process takes overnight only to mature. Just as it takes time for a person to learn new things or even build your muscles, so it requires time in developing self-discipline. For instance, if you are aiming at building muscles, you will need to take your time and train more. The more you engage in training, the more likely you will build your muscles and become strong. However, if your goal is to achieve a muscular body at once, you will be discouraged because it is not practical. Overworking yourself will only lead to setbacks due to injuries.

The same case applies when you aim at building your self-esteem. You will need to go through each step at a time in order to achieve your dreams. Therefore, the first step is to make the decision to progress and ensure you learn what is required to get to that destination. If you don't follow step by step towards gaining self-discipline, you will be overwhelmed when you experience too many changes you need to make at once. In the end, this may kill your intention of becoming self-disciplined.

Know What Motivates You and What Demotivates You

The first step in gaining self-discipline is to know and discover yourself. Sometimes it is easy to find we are being overcome by cravings and urges and so knowing areas in your life where you have no power no resist and avoid it will significantly help. For instance, if you know you can't avoid junks or other deep-fried foods, it will be advisable to stay away from them. Ensure you stay away from them to prevent them from luring you during the times of weakness.

Also, if you are aware that no matter how much pressure you put on yourself, it does not work, then you should put yourself in an environment that will promote the building of self-discipline as compared to a situation that will sabotage it. Stay away from temptations and stay close to items that soothe and encourage you such as motivating slogans and images of what you wish to attain.

It is essential to know what empowers and motivates you. Your will power will be directly proportional to your energy levels, and so you could play energetic songs to raise you up and laugh. Make yourself love what you are doing by staying energized. This will make it possible to put in place desirable and appropriate behaviors in your daily routine – which is what self-discipline entails.

Ensure Some Behaviors Are Your Routine

When you have settled on what is most important to you and what goals to put your effort on, have a daily routine that will enable you to attain them. For example, if you are working towards eating healthily or even losing weight, decide to take several servings of vegetables and fruits every day and do exercises for about thirty minutes a day. Ensure your daily habit is promoting the development of self-discipline. Consequently, you should keep away from bad, self-defeating practices, all that they may be. These practices can put you in a negative state of mind and derail your self-discipline. Also, avoid possessing a poor attitude because it is also a bad habit.

Exercise Self-Denial

When you are on a journey to developing self-discipline, you should learn to restrict some feelings, urges, and impulses. Train to act on what you believe is right, even if it is against you will. Skip some desserts on some evenings, limit your watching, and restrict yourself from yelling at anyone who irritates you. Always stop and think before you take steps and think about the outcomes of any action that you take. When you embrace the practice of self-restraint, it will enable you to promote a habit of keeping all things under control.

Involve Yourself in Sporting and Other Activities

Engaging in sports activities is among one of the best ways to promote self-discipline. Sports will train you to put in place your goals, focus both your emotional and mental energies, be fit physically and can get well along with others. Involving yourself in sports offers a situation where you work harder and put all your effort which in turn will enable you to integrate the same thought processes and discipline in your daily life.

Also practicing playing instruments to music can be another better way to practice self-discipline. There is an invaluable effort, repetition and application needed to when learning to play these instruments. When you attain self-discipline in any area, it will help reprogram your minds, and it will be easy to choose what is right instead of going for what is easy.

Get Inspired from The Right Places

There are many people out there who have achieved self-discipline and so learning from them will save a great deal. Be it in athletics, or any activity that you have decided to involve yourself in, make sure you are inspired by the people you admire. You should have a strong desire to do the right thing and go out of your way to achieve it. Some of the challenges you are facing today, have been experienced many people who have experienced the same and overcome and developing self-discipline is not exceptional.

Focus on The Rewards

There is nothing that brings a lot of satisfaction like accomplishing what you had aimed for. Exercise the techniques that high achievers and athletes' practice. See yourself in the future with your desired outcomes. You will see the benefits that you will get and always remind yourself of the price you ought to pay for you to get there.

Overcoming Temptation as A Foundation for Success

As you go through the past and review your goals, be keen to look at what has held you back from achieving your goals. One important question that you ought to ask yourself is what temptations you gave into. How can you stop yourself from letting temptations deter you from your goals?

Temptation can be defined as the desire to do something, particularly something wrong or unwise. It can also be a thing or course of actions that can attract or tempt you. This implies that once you have purposed to do something, for instance losing weight- you will meet every kind of temptation from every corner. You may go out with your friends for a party and have a glass of wine and skipping your gym sessions. You may even be finding yourself tempted to grab that piece of donut or cookies in the kitchen. Often our temptation is so habitual and usually unnoticed now, that you can quickly forget your focus goal. It is paramount for you to understand that these little amounts of food we need now or skipping the gym do not add anything towards where we aim to be. It is easy to get distracted that we fail to realize the temptations that face us.

The temptation that we face every day make us far from what we truly want. However, those temptations can make you strong when we push and refuse to give in to them. It is easy to be tempted to stray. The challenge comes when we decide to remain stronger.

Many times, at the start of your goal, you will strive to keep going. At that moment the temptation is stronger. When you experience the first signs of results, momentum will start to kick in; you will have more ability to fight temptation. Always remember that you are stronger than both the temptation and the will to give in. Human beings sometimes need to be challenged so that they can bring out their best.

How Do Temptations Work Against Your Goals?

It is important to note that all temptations follow a four-step process. It is paramount to learn it so that we can start being keen to where we might get caught by it.

A Desire That Comes from Within or A Feeling

Sometimes you might have a strong desire to revenge, control a situation or other people. It might even be an urge to feel appreciated or have pleasure. Many times, temptation begins in the mind. It is easy for you to negative minds, which can make it hard to achieve your targets. You might tell yourself – "it's only once", "it is good to go out with friends or colleagues because it will it will be fun", and the likes. This temptation will always start with your minds. Something will always be pushing us away from our objective or intentions. The circumstances that we found ourselves is not to blame for falling into temptation but our minds. Your mind will tell you it is okay if you do certain things. Therefore, for you to avoid giving in to temptation, you must start being cautious from the thoughts and imaginations that pulls you away from what you have planned.

Starting to Doubt

Sometimes you might find yourself doubting what you know. Your mind might tell you that skipping one day at the gym will not make a huge difference or I will take a day off because tomorrow I will get more work done. Your mind will argue that you deserve to be happy and to have what makes you happy, so go for it. Always be careful not to start doubting what you know. You should set your mind to fight the feeling of doubt. Remind yourself what you know and believe. For instance, remind yourself that skipping the gym for one day might make you lazy to do exercises the following day, having a day off today does not imply that tomorrow you will work extra hard or, eating sugar today might make you crave for more sugar. When you remind yourself of these things, you will not allow your minds to give in easily.

Be on The Lookout for Deception

You should remain alert lest your minds start lying to you. Remember you will always battle with temptations. Your thoughts might be tempted to think that all will be okay, you won't notice that one day off when you are being paid, everybody else is doing the same thing, or nobody will ever notice or know. Remember the saying what is done in the darkness will eventually reveal itself at a time. If you aim to lose weight and gain that impressive figure that you so much desire, you should stop eating the wrong diet if though you are tempted to do so. You are smart and have the power within you, and therefore you should not give in to that feeling that is whispering lies to you.

You Start Disobeying

If you give in to the three above, temptation has won. You will give in and begin doing things that will keep you away from your goals.

It is like a cycle. When you have sat down and review your goal for a week, month or year, ask yourself- what temptation have you fallen into? Which are the cravings and desires that arose? How did doubt manifest itself? What lies have you convinced yourself that it was fine? How long did it take for you to give in to temptation? For instance, it may be that you have purposed not to spend on a month, and you are able to keep that in the first week, but you have this strong desire to buy a smartphone you have been seeing. You don't obtain it in the first week, and you stay committed to what you had purposed. But as days go, doubt starts to rise, your mind starts telling you that if you buy this, it will give you immeasurable benefits and that it remains a viable "investment". You start arguing that not having it is bad and you begin lying to yourself.

Your minds will tell you that since in the last two weeks you didn't spend any money you can now afford this. You start forgetting your bigger plan of saving money and not spending during the month. The temptation is drawing your minds to doubt your decision of "not getting it now". You are tempted to believe it is okay and finally, before the end of the month, you give and buy it. In this time although it took some time, temptation won.

Temptations can also deter us from our goals very easy. For instance, you may bump into your friends in a party and find everyone holding a glass of wine, and you grab the glass and start drinking. In this situation, the thought got into your minds very quickly as you saw the wine. It was easy for you to doubt that this would make a difference in your diet. Your mind will tell you it is only one and then I will stay clear from such for the rest of the day. Sadly, here temptation won in just a few minutes.

Start reviewing your goals and look at what temptations you tend to give in. See whether it relates to people or situations? Is it when you are stressed? Can you visualize your goal? What is pulling you back? Create a journal list concerning it and pay close attention to you and your actions. Know how easily you give in to the four steps. This will be the start to fight your temptation.

Developing Willpower as A Foundation for Success

Willpower can be termed as having the ability to resist short term temptations so that you can achieve your long-term goals. It is the ability to delay your gratification for a specific purpose. Human beings use will power in one way or the other in their everyday life; it may be when resisting the craving to eat sweets or desisting from browsing the internet when there are tasks to be achieved.

It is no doubt that willpower plays an important role in determining whether you will achieve your goals or not. In fact, lack of willpower may be the major hindrance from having good behaviors. Having strong willpower will enable you to achieve more in school, in your career and your personal life.

In life, those people who can delay their gratification have a better chance of having a chance to get into competitive environments and perform better. It is my view that self-discipline and willpower are more important than IQ when one is determined to gain outstanding success.

A very thin line separates success and failure. We can easily succumb to temptation when we are on the verge of succeeding and leave your goal unaccomplished. The presence or lack of willpower will be instrumental in determining if we achieve or fail to attain the set targets. There is a soul in the human body that controls the intellect and mind and gives the mind the ability to overcome the negative characteristics and impulses like inaction, laziness, depression, and procrastination.

People easily become weak in their urge for willpower, and their self-confidence begins to reduce. A great way to improve your willpower is to adhere to a routine of yoga and meditation. During meditation, you will have a state of no-thought that will lead to emptiness which will be instrumental in knowing yourself and discovering the truth. Also, fasting is another way that will help develop willpower. Fasting will not only detoxify the system but will also train you to endure and give you a spirit of self-control and acceptance.

Procrastination

Although it is right to make thoughtful decisions, taking a lot of time to think before getting to a decision can be very bad for any person especially if you are responsible for leadership. When you become too slow to act, react, communicate and make decisions, you are on the verge of failing. Success is always time conscious especially in the current world where there is a lot of competition. People are bound to make decisions swiftly so that they can align themselves to act on what they have purposed.

Whether it is in leadership or in your personal life, you should not take an eternity to decide as this will impact negatively on the outcomes. We all find ourselves procrastinating at a point in our lives and is a mistake that is very easy to make. Failure to make good and swift decisions when we are faced with a crisis can lead to worst consequences.

For everybody, here are some reasons it's important to make decisions quickly:

Time Could Work Against You

It is common for human beings to think that conditions don't change and whatever the decision you must take can wait for some time until you have done all considerations. But that is not always the case only very few things will stay static in this ever-changing world. There are some situations where waiting can work to your advantage. For instance, you may be thinking to fire one of your staffs, -but after taking time without firing him, he decides to resign.

However, many times we will be forced to act very fast and decide rather than waiting for the situation to determine our fate. Making your decision swiftly means that you are in control of what is going around you and within you. Through this, you will be able to take measures that will ensure that you are not caught up amid controversies.

When You Fail to Respond You Will Face Huge Problems as Compared If You Had Responded

Many people learn this the hard way. Some individuals will delay until when people are fed up and have started complaining before taking actions. As a leader, you should not wait until when people have begun holding rallies and demonstrations for you to engage them in communication or handle their grievances. Sometimes it may too late and getting things together again may not be possible.

When you don't procrastinate upon decisions, you will have enough time to do your consultations, and if there is a need for you to apologize, you will do it. You may at times find yourself in a place where your apology will not be taken in good faith because you stayed long before delivering your apology. This might cost you your career or even lose several the closest people in your life.

When You Make Your Decisions Late, You Will Affect People in Ways You Could Not Anticipate

You should not think that you know how people will react when you decide late. People respond differently when subjected to unexpected announcements. For example, when I was at college, the management of the school decided to stop providing our payments towards the expenses on health plan until 5 hours when those plans were to expire. The funny thing is that the university knew that the decision had been overturned more than one month ago but delayed until the last moment to inform us.

You can tell what followed next after this last-minute announcement – the whole institution backfired. We walked out, and the administration was forced to overturn its ruling and eventually paid its share of the health plans through fellowships. If they had told us in advance, they could not have experienced that unfriendly situation, and maybe they could have gotten away with it.

Only A Few Decisions Are Not Reversible

Sometimes a lot of people procrastinate because they think that the kind of decision, they will make is not reversible. However, it is good to understand that most decisions that you can make can be altered later. Most people may see you as a flip-flopper, but by providing a clear explanation of what led you to change your mind is likely to silence your critics. In my opinion, it is much better to flip-flop instead of doing nothing at all.

It Gives You Time to Apologize and Reconcile

When you make timely decisions, and in any case, they cause friction among your colleagues, you will have time to apologize and get everyone on board again. Apologizing is a powerful tool to diffuse even fiercest critics and gain respect from some of them. Therefore, acting on time will not only mean that you will have things done on time but also give you an opportunity to apologize if things go amiss.

Chapter 2:
Self-Discipline Fundamentals

All of us wish to have success in our lives. Maybe you are trying to lose weight or succeed in business. But have you ever asked yourself why achieving weight or succeeding in business or career is not possible for most people? Did you find a convincing reason? If not, stay on because in this chapter we shall help you unravel how commitment and believing in yourself are key fundamental in losing weight and the success of your business.

Most people have attempted to lose weight at a point in their life. Some were not successful because they did not stay committed while others did not believe that their plan was going to work. Others wish that they could become world-class business people but don't start any business, and so their business idea remains just on their minds. Always note that although all things start as an idea in our minds, for you to achieve your set goals, you should be involved and commit yourself to a plan of self-empowerment and have a great conviction that your plan is going to work.

The first step towards success in life is staying committed. To better explain this, I will use dieting as an example. Losing weight may seem like a simple thing, but for you to achieve it, you will need to exercise a high level of commitment. Most individuals trying to lose weight are not consistent with the right practices that would help them to lose weight. Most of them usually start well and appear to show results during the first days after they have started. However, very few achieve their long-term goals of losing weight. The reason is that most people do not know the secret of staying committed.

For you to lose a substantial amount of weight in the long-term, you should be able to maintain a certain weight loss for over five years. Always stay committed and engage in high-level physical activities, eat a diet with low calories and maintain a consistent eating pattern all days.

Sometimes after you have just started on your journey to lose weight, you may not realize that you are losing weight. It is normal for you not to see any difference on the scale during the first days or weeks, but this should not make you worried that you aren't losing fat. The bodyweight usually tends to change by only a few pounds. The foods that you take are the primary determinants, and sometimes the hormones can have a big impact on the level of water your body can retain (particularly in women). Therefore, when you don't notice a huge change in your scale don't give up yet but rather stay committed and stay put in your plan.

For you to enjoy a long-term weight loss success, you should experience a maintained weight loss for a duration between two and five years. After this duration, you will have a higher chance of having long term success. During these 2 to 5 years, what happens is that your daily commitment to follow a certain plan each day will transform into long-term self-discipline.

When you are overweight and have decided to lose weight, you should pick the right diet that makes sense to you especially a low-carb diet and stay on it for several months. Learn all the guidelines and follow them. If you take those guidelines seriously, you will be surprised at how much weight you can lose in the long-term, and unlike most first-time dieters, you will achieve your goal right away. Some people tend to try over ten different diets before achieving weight loss but with commitment and believing in your plan, it is possible to hit your target in about three months with trying other diets. Once you change your habits and stick with them, you will be amazed at how easy you can maintain a healthy weight.

Staying committed to your plan means you will carefully keep track of what you are eating. Being cautious of what you are eating and what you should not is very important. You might argue that many individuals who don't lose weight are not careful on the type of food they are eating. But the secret to losing weight is not majorly the type of food that you eat but rather being able to commit to it and believe that it will bring the result you expect. The key to losing and maintaining weight is having the ability to follow a plan and stick to it until you attain your intended goals. When I was 25 years, I was overweight by about 20 pounds. When I decided to cut some weight, I choose a diet that I felt it could help me. I adhered to it for some months, but when I noticed that I was losing some weight, I started changing my diet.

I realized that when I stopped being committed to my plan and started doubting it, I started gaining weight again. Just like most first-time dieters, I did not experience success immediately. I tried various diets and could not achieve my goals. When I talked to my nutritionist, he was shocked to hear that I had changed my diet several times. I was advised on the need of staying committed to my plan and believe that it would work. I stopped returning to my old ways and practices, and I am to say that after I had altered my practices and adhered to them, I was able to maintain a healthy weight.

You can't have that business success that you so much desire without commitment and believing in yourself. Today there is more and more business drafted than before, but do all these proposals see the light of the day? Are you among those individuals that wake every morning and imagine the great opportunities that life has to offer and do nothing? Success in any area of your life and particularly in business is earned and not something you can obtain by wishing only. This reminds me of a common saying that goes " if wishes were horses beggars would ride". Have you ever asked yourself what commitments some of the greatest billionaires in the USA and around the world have made so that they can possess the kind of success they have? Don't worry you will get your answer below.

One crucial thing you should note is that the kind of commitment you have will determine how successful you will become. It is shocking that a lot of individuals usually stop at the "wish" point and don't purpose to endure the struggle and commit to their goals. This is the main reason that makes most people not to succeed. You cannot have a short path to success; you can only attain success through staying committed and believing that your plan is going to work. The path to success is not as smooth as it may look. Otherwise, we would all be successful. You must make a lot of sacrifices so that you can have a life that you have always dreamed of.

Some of the Commitments Essential for Your Success

#1 Commitment: Belief in Yourself

Before other people begin to believe in you, you must believe in yourself. Whatever the dreams you have, be sure to believe in them and trust that you have what it takes to accomplish them. What happens with most people is that they highly underestimate their abilities, and this becomes the main hindrance to discovering their potential.

Note down all your strengths, greatest achievements, uniqueness and accomplishments and remind yourself of them each morning. This can greatly help in strengthening belief in yourself. Most people have much potential, but they are drawn back by having low self-esteem. The important thing is to believe in yourself and your abilities.

#2 Commitment: Acting Massively Daily

After you have decided on what you want to pursue in life, put in place an action plan towards it. Regardless of whether you have set small or huge goals, there is need to commit yourself to act each day massively without excuses.

The first step to involve yourself in towards this is to ensure your minds are prepared to chase your goals passionately. Start by having a plan. While there are many planning tools to assist you in making your plan, be sure to customize your plan to be line with your needs and abilities. Be very realistic while doing this so that you will remain inspired to take the necessary actions each day without fail.

#3 Commitment: Be Adaptive and Learn Always

Being able to adapt and passionate can lead you to greater levels in life. It is surprising that some individuals are so rigid in their minds that they usually reject any suggestions given to them. This can be so detrimental to both their professional and general life.

Charles Darwin said, " It is not the strongest of the species that survives, not even the most intelligent that survives. It is the one that is the most adaptable to change."

Therefore, it is important that you learn from those that you desire as this is something that can impact positively in life. Learn continually without stopping because in many cases there are several ways of handling the same issue. When you change your mind and learn to adapt, you will see more chances in ways that you have never imagined.

#4 Commitment: Be Willing to Lose Sleep and Say NO

People who experience success are those people who are willing to take any step to attain success. You will not only need to work hard, but you will also need to say no to some things that do not go in line with your goals and dreams. It is gratifying and tempting to spend time with your friends for a party or shopping but staying committed on your startup or revising a blog you had written is what would make you experience a real difference. If you are held up in your job during the daytime, the only time you can pursue your own dreams is working during the night, which means thus you will sacrifice some hours of your sleep.

Another way to show commitment in your goals is by saying NO. sometimes it may be challenging to say NO to friends, but by doing so you will start experiencing more success and happiness than other people who have no courage to say NO.

#5 Commitment: Avoid Immoral or Unethical Stuff

You can achieve success through two different ways: an easy way or a difficult way. When you take an easy way, it means that you will do anything to get there

– by hook or by crook. This implies that you will take shortcuts, practice unethical things, receiving favors just for the sake of achieving your goal. However, commitment does not involve in any of the above.

It is easy to get seduced to do unethical stuff so that you can have quick results. However, it is good to note that quick results come with a price and can easily ruin you in a short time. Always know that the journey towards success will test your character together with dedication.

#6 Commitment: Proper Work and Life Balance

If you didn't know the most single most important thing in your life is your health. Both your mental and physical health play a significant role in your life because all things are either directly or indirectly dependent on your health.

You should entertain a habit of working hard for so many hours that you forget how important your health is. If for instance, you have worked for 30 good hours, it is good to allow your body rest as it deserves. If working even during the weekends, find a time to relax with people close to you so that you can feel refreshed.

#7 Commitment: Never Give Up

This may sound like a cliché, but ever giving up especially on yourself is the blocker to success. When walking through life, falling is inevitable. There are times when your falling will be due to some of the mistakes you have done, and it is okay. Life has many unexpected occurrences, but you should never allow this to affect your spirit negatively in any manner.

Always be reminded that for you to achieve and tap your best potential, you will need a lot of faith. This spirit will enable you when you are going through tough times. Don't fail to believe that your plan will work.

Commitment means staying loyal to what you said you will do even after the mood that you said it in is gone. Now, it is up to you to decide to stay committed and take actions or let situations control you.

Chapter 3:
Habits of Winners

Self-discipline is at the mind and heart of any successful individual. Whether this is a success in their professional or personal life, it all begins with an inner ability to have self-control though discipline. For you to have that success that you are admiring you must put your minds, emotions, habits, and behaviors under check.

If you in dire need of achieving those great goals that you have set, it is paramount that you understand how self-discipline having is a crucial ingredient to your success journey. The best thing is that self-discipline is not a new thing in the world. In fact, there has been a long-time discussion concerning self-discipline, and it has been exhibited by some of the most successful persons in the world. Our ability to succeed is in any area of our life is majorly dependent on the right habits that we form while still young. However, you cannot achieve those good habits without having the ability to discipline your behaviors and actions. I am a strong believer of the fact that with self-discipline, almost everything is possible. You will be amazed at how much confidence you will gain through being self-disciplined.

Most successful people have attributed their success to self-discipline and believe that self-control is the gateway to achieving any goal in life. For the sake of your success, you must learn how to make use of self-discipline in your life to achieve your goals. Successful people have leveraged on this art of self-discipline through setting a foundational set of good behaviors that allowed to see things the others could not see.

Many may ask how self-discipline is attained or created? What makes one individual have what looks like total control of their actions and habits, while others try but fail? How is it possible for one individual to be very keen on the actions they take every day, while others don't? The answer to these concerns is based on the habits. Since about forty oy your behavior is determined by habit, it is essential to check on your habits for you to attain self-discipline.

Let us look at habits are key to self-discipline. When you practice the below habits, you can have a good foundation within which you can achieve your dreams. Without possessing these habits and actions, it will be like you are chasing the wind which is merely impossible.

Habits: The Foundation to Self-Discipline

Having that what we do most every day is based on our habit, developing the right habit will be instrumental in having the right levels of discipline in our lives. One may be asking, where do habits originate from and through which ways can you achieve them? And what makes us when we strive to alter our habits through either breaking our bad behaviors or exercising the right habits, we are only able to follow that route for a certain period before going back to our former ways?

The greatest challenge, particularly with habits and actions that most people have experienced for a long time is that the minds are used to neural pathways. Neural pathways are required when linking neural networks for a specific function like going up the stairs, smoking, or when preparing something in a certain manner.

Neural pathways allow behavior automation that is repeated constantly with an aim to minimize conscious power of processing in mind. This will, in turn, allow your mind to concentrate on anything else that might be happening. This is built from when we are young and makes part of our genetic makeup and allows the mind to be more efficient so that it can be used in many other things.

However, in most cases, repeated normal behaviors tend to hold us back. In most cases, we have a lot of bad habits that impact negatively on our lives as compared to possessing good habits that could push us forward.

However, instilling the following habits in life, you will discover that achieving the self-discipline will be much easier. Again, you should note that either forming or breaking a habit will take time.

Gratitude

Do you find yourself spending much of your time wishing for things? Then having the habit of gratitude can significantly help you to move from constantly wishing for what you lack and instead appreciate what you have. When you exercise this, you will notice significant shifts beginning to happen. Gratitude has far-reaching impacts. They ranginess from having improved mental health, to your emotional wellbeing, to your spirituality. Gratitude can bring a lot of changes in you, but most importantly it allows you to move from the state of scarcity to a state of abundance.

When you live in a state of lack, it becomes nearly impossible to work on being self-disciplined and attaining your goals. You will spend most of your time worrying concerning what we lack and live in a state of fear, always forgetting what we possess. When you live in a state of lack for long, it can easily lead to physical issues. It may lead to the production of stress hormones like cortisol and epinephrine, which can affect many parts of your body.

As part of promoting self-discipline, spend about 5-10 minutes and see the things you are thankful about. You may see as if there is nothing for you to show gratitude for but search for it.

Meditation

Meditation is key in helping your minds be at peace. It gives you spiritual centeredness that gives room for growth. When you in meditation, you stay clear of all the noise and discover that you are among the beings in the universe that are well connected. Also, meditation is an important key when you are trying to promote self-discipline. It helps clear your mind palette and gives you the best tone for the day. It is instrumental in allowing you to have an improved emotional, mental, spiritual and physical health, allowing you to have huge benefits within a short time.

You don't require much time for you to meditate. You can do it in about ten minutes. You only need to ensure that your minds are quiet and don't allow them to wander. When you notice your mind begins to wander, reel them back. Ensure your energy is grounded in the earth, open your palms while facing the heavens and make sure you are feeling the air when breathing in and out.

Because meditation involves aligning the physical body with your spiritual, it allows you to live a focused life with no worries concerning common issues that usually brings people down. In simple terms, it makes your load light.

Nutrition

Did you know that your body spends about 10-25% of your energy to process and digest food? When you take a diet that is rich in fats, carbohydrates or even proteins, your body will spend a lot of energy in processing that food, and sadly much of those foods will not be helpful to us.

Both raw food and fruits will give the greatest boost for energy as they need less energy during processing and surprisingly will provide more energy for your body to use.

The kind of energy you have within you plays a significant role in determining how focused you will be. When you are focused, you can face your dreams with a lot of discipline. On the other hand, when you are negatively affected by the food that you have taken, it will not be easy to achieve discipline. You will spend a lot of your time feeling sluggish to get anything accomplished.

Therefore, purpose to eat healthy food during breakfast and any other meal of the day. For you to attain this, you must plan on what to eat and restrict yourself from bad habits. Avoid fast foods because they will not give you the energy that your body requires to face your dreams with discipline. Also, food can alter the neurochemical composition of your brain, which has a significant influence on the connection between your body and mind. Go for raw, healthy and organic foods if possible and avoid taking junk foods.

Sleep

Sleep is directly related to your ability to stay disciplined. Getting the right amount of sleep is important to ensuring anything is done. When you don't get enough sleep for a long time, it will affect your mood, your ability to focus, your judgment, your nutrition and your health in general. In fact, when you deprive yourself of sleep for an extended period, things might get out of hand for you as this can cause certain diseases and affect your immune system.

Sleeping for 6-8 hours is important no matter how busy you may be. Also, avoid drinking a lot of caffeinated drinks for a minimum of five hours before you go to bed because caffeine can interfere with your natural sleeping cycle. During the day, it is advisable to avoid too many toxins from cigarettes, alcohol and some medications if possible.

Generally, benefits that come from having enough sleep are more. Despite helping you be more disciplined, you will have improved memory, restrain inflammation and pain, reduce stress, promote your creativity, make your more attentive and limit your chances of being depressed.

Exercise Regularly

Having a habit of exercising regularly is a significant key to self-discipline. It provides a foundation to a life full of good and positive actions, free from wrong habits. Do you really aspire to discipline yourself? Practice the key habit of exercising daily in your mornings. Although benefits that come from exercising regularly are immeasurable, most people have not yet purposed to make exercise a priority in their daily routines.

While most people are running up and down during the day to get things done, they are making a huge mistake by not doing exercises. Most people argue that they can't be able to put up with this habit or that they have a lot to handle instead of exercising. But that is where they get it wrong.

When you embrace this key of regular exercise, you will not only become more disciplined, but you will also find your life improved in many ways. First, exercising regularly will help minimize the levels of stress and pain when it releases endorphins and neurotransmitters like dopamine and serotonin.

Secondly, exercise regularly will enhance your health by enhancing the flow of blood and increase oxygen in the body cells and ultimately help the body fight diseases and improve your immune system. Again, exercise will help you to remain more focused on a task and enabling you to live a life full of discipline. When instilling the habit of regular exercise in your life, begin small. You can start by having a walk in the morning for five minutes. When you have done that for about a week, you can then increase that to ten or more minutes for another week. As you on with this pattern for more weeks increasing bit by bit, you will realize that you have created a habit without much struggle.

Forgiveness

When most of your days are filled with anger, guilt, and regret, we experience more problems than solutions. In fact, you will need more energy to sustain hate and anger as opposed to when exercising love and forgiveness. When you learn to forgive, you will be able to let some things go. It is hard for you to achieve self-discipline without exercising a habit of forgiveness. This is because most of the time you will be worried about how so and so wronged you that you fail to concentrate on your important goals like achieving self-discipline.

If you have been wronged by a person or a group of people, try and forgive. This does not basically mean that you forget. It only means that you will not unnecessary energy holding grudges. When you forgive, you are letting go of the negativity that deters from achieving self-discipline--trying to discipline yourself? Forgiveness gives you a major avenue. Although it may not initially appear like a habit of discipline, it remains among the most significant ones.

I cannot promise you that it is easy to forgive but looking at the benefits that you will benefit personally after you have forgiven, it is worth doing it. Think about all the people that have longed you and find a reason to forgive. One of the ways to forgive them is to put yourself in their place and think if you could have done differently if you were in their situation. Look for humor and find a lesson that you learned from what happened.

It is until you let go of those bad feelings towards other people that most things in your life will start improving. Restrain yourself from being worried and being stressed so that you can move forward towards self-discipline.

Be Organized

For you to attain self-disciplined and succeed in your dreams, you must be organized. Being organized is a habit that you need to fully incorporate no just in your professional life but also in your personal life. This means that you must keep both your home and office organized in line with things in your minds. You can't have an organized life minus discipline – they are intertwined. If you are disorganized, you will need to start small as you improve each day. You can organize one small space in the kitchen on the first day, while the following day you move to organize your bedroom.

Just like any other habit, you will need patience so that the habit of organization can be built. You will need to put some effort and be attentive, but after some time, you will see the benefits. When you have organized the physical space surrounding you, your mind will relax, stress will reduce, and you will be more focused.

Ultimately, it is easy to gain more self-discipline when you have an organized life. This entails that you will put anything in its right place when you are through using it. It's the small things that you do each day that largely impacts on the kind of life that you live. Always be attentive to small things in life, and you will benefit largely.

Persistence

My list of habits that are key for self-discipline would be incomplete without persistence. Persistence is needed if you are to go through tough situations and not give up. It also helps you in the case that you fail or fall you get back to your feet and push forward. Without being persistent, it would be almost impossible to achieve self-discipline. The reason I say this is because achieving your goals is not easy. It is easy to get discouraged and give up that staying put and pushing forward particularly if by pushing forward you are experiencing pain or discomfort.

The point to take note of here is that even the most successful individuals that we admire and see them as role models have gone through failure multiple times. Failure is important in pushing our determination forward, and without it, we could not achieve some of the goals that we put in place.

Chapter 4:
Millionaire Self-Discipline Secrets

Sometimes back I was experimenting a crazy diet where I fasted for 18 hours and only ate the food that I admired for the six hours. I was introduced to this diet by one of my workout partners and what I realized while I was on this plan is that I had unusual urge to take snacks at midnight or a meal at around three in the morning. It was a challenge to stay without having a bite from my hidden packet of chips. I know this is a common battle to you too, where you find yourself fighting with your inner critic where you have one side arguing it is okay to give in to the wrong side whereas the other try to convince you not to break the promise or target you set for yourself. Many times, you may find yourself experiencing struggles that lead to a major conflict in your minds. You may be struggling to lose weight, but you have the unfortunate urge pushing you away from exercising. You don't know how valuable your couch is to you until you start having the idea to work out.

The reason you find self-discipline, so challenging is because it demands your conscious to act in a certain manner regardless of what your emotions are. It is common when waking up in the morning for your emotions to try and convince you to stay in the best and snooze the alarm. But you must apply your conscious minds that tell that it is wrong to miss work or school that will enable you to move out of your comfort zone. This happens to me frequently, especially on Mondays. I am always tempted to snooze the alarm and go back to sleep instead of going to work. Was it not for my conscious telling me that my boss will not tolerate me missing for work; I could easily give in.?

I know you are asking yourself, why is it too hard to have self-discipline throughout when we are trying to accomplish our goals? Why are we not able to follow to the goals that we set our minds onto daily? Most challenges that people face are as a result of our failure to maintain self-discipline. From harmful addictions, overeating, debts, and laziness have greatly impacted negatively to our economy.

In your day to day activities, you use willpower, either knowingly or unknowingly. The mistake that is common to most people is that when they hear about self-discipline, they think that it only applies to major tasks that they have yet to do. However, you need to apply self-discipline even in smaller tasks like refusing the temptation to eat a donut in the morning. You use willpower when you decide not to get upset after you are caught in a snarl-up on your way to work or even you when you decide not to fight a person who embarrasses you. Without much ado, look at the below mind tricks that will help you master self-discipline:

Eat More Often

I know this may sound weird, but it is one of the tricks you can use to master your discipline. Your brain is a power-plant that requires regular replenishment. Individuals that always starve themselves have shown to have low self-discipline as compared to those who eat regularly. However, this does not necessarily mean that you should be overeating as that would lead to the development of unnatural bad habits. This means that your body requires a steady glucose level which helps give energy to the brains and other vital body organs.

In simple terms, glucose acts as fuel to your brains so that they can work perfectly. When you have a low level of glucose in your blood, you are prone to making poor judgments that may lead to regrets in the coming days. Therefore, it is good to begin your day with a healthy breakfast or eat a light meal before undergoing a test. If you experience instances when you feel irritated, take something small. On my case, having fruits, a light meal or even a drink saves me a great deal.

The only caution you should take when eating is to avoid taking unhealthy foods. Sometimes you may even be forced to stay away from environments where such foods are found.

Handle One Goal at a Time

What has made a lot of people fail to accomplish their goals is handling so many tasks at a go. This makes it hard for them to stay committed in any of them. This is the same mistake people make when setting up the New Year's resolutions. Sometimes you may start a project out of excitement, but as time goes, you may realize that you put yourself in so much work. It may make you get worn out and drained, and you may find yourself losing interest on the project as you had before.

To ensure you have maintained self-discipline in your mind, ensure you work on each goal at a given time. This will enable you to maintain your willpower more easily because you will not be overwhelmed with so many tasks that would add up on the way.

Have A Strong Believe About Willpower

A person's willpower is directly proportional to their beliefs. This means if an individual had low-level willpower, they would be met by limited possibilities. On the other hand, if a person had strong willpower, it will not be easy to get exhausted before achieving their goals. Although there are still ongoing engagements among scientists concerning the willpower, a lot of suggestions are showing that the concept you have towards willpower will come true.

When you have a limited belief, you are always going to experience obstacles on your way which will be your limitations. Before realizing it, you will have already set your mind to fail. This means that for you to succeed, you will require a huge boost in motivation.

Use Rewards

Our minds work in a way that they work towards something. When you set rewards for yourself when you achieve something, you will be motivated to work much harder towards achieving it. You may be arguing, but I have huge aspirations, do I still to motivate myself through rewards? Yes, because in some cases you may feel like what you are doing is not worth and therefore using rewards means you will see what you are doing is worth doing.

You can set yourself mind in a way that you will only get a certain reward after you are through with a task. This will help you reinforce yourself and become a more disciplined person.

Put in Place Alternatives or Backup Plan

This means taking situations that you usually face and have an alternative way out of it. For example, let's say you are working towards eating healthy, and you find yourself in a party with your buddies. You should have an answer to let's say a person offers you fatty foods. You should deny it and instead ask for your favorite drink instead or even water. This will allow you to have a self-intended mindset instead of jumping into situations blindly. This will prevent you from making wrong choices based on majority or the state of your emotions.

No one knows you like yourself in the world. You know your strengths and your habits. So, for you to ensure you don't fall on bad traits, have an alternative way to get out of it. Remind yourself how you would act if you knew the obstacles heading your way. If you know it's hard for you to exercise when you arrive home, have a plan to do nothing else when you get home before doing your exercises. When you have a plan for you to follow, there are higher chances that you will achieve it.

Don't Allow Yourself to Be Distracted

Out of sight out of mind rule will significantly help here. This is a powerful way to master your self-discipline by avoiding temptations that can disembark you from your goals. When you are constantly surrounded by things that cause you temptation, it will lead to unnecessary battles in the minds. Sometimes you may find yourself battling whether you should take candy in the bowl resting on the table or not. When you experience these hard decisions, your skills for making decisions and energy will be drained. This energy is required for you to make good decisions.

If you know you have other things to deal with in the house, avoid unnecessary temptations like the internet and television. An effective way to avoid internet is to stay away from major social networks and continue with your work. Through this, you will have strong willpower to do your assignments with little or no interruptions at all.

Assess Your Ability to Withstand Pain

The foundation of self-discipline lies in having the ability to overcome pain. Know how much suffering you are willing to take in order to achieve your goals. Always note that not everything is worth suffering for, and not every suffering produces results. Begin the day by asking yourself ``what suffering am I willing to go through today?" be honest to yourself because we all have a limit to our pain tolerance. Being honest will enable you to find ways to achieve goals that are in line with your limits.

Most people fail because they make the mistake of overestimating their limits. What this means is that when they are subjected to difficult situations, they will find it hard to withstand until they can achieve their goals.

Ensure Consistency

If you are the kind of person who makes excuses on almost everything you will neither attain self-discipline nor be happy. You must not allow yourself to make excuses concerning your kids or lack of time. Always find time for what is important to you. Be it is daily on monthly start small and keep going. Commit yourself no matter how hard and rough it may seem.

If you have purposed to go to the gym for the purpose of losing weight, don't allow anything to push you back. Perform your exercises daily. You can start with a ten minutes' walk during the first week as you increase by 5 minutes each week. Through this you will remain consistent and achieving your goal will be easy. You cannot achieve self-discipline without consistency.

Employ Muscle-Building Skills in Decision Making

Building self-discipline works the same way as heading to the gym to build muscles. This means that the more you practice it, the firm it becomes. A good starting place is to visualize how perfect you will get things done, imagine and have a mental picture of the advantages and satisfaction you will have once you have accomplished them. When you have a clear vision of your goal in your head, you will be motivated.

Monitoring Your Progress

After you have in place a clear goal, a better way to ensure you remain committed is to monitor your progress frequently. Some individuals will not, however, require a tracker because they spent a very long-time mastering both their willingness and self-discipline. However, for those starting, it is important to keep track of each step they are making towards their goals because of failure to that they may give up and ultimately forget.

When you have a journal of your actions, you will realize that tracking your work will help you how much you have accomplished. This will make you proud when you discover what you have achieved by the end of the day. Although you may not have attained your dreams, you will see how close you are each day.

Chapter 5:
The Fool Proof Method to Achieve Your Goals

Self-control, also called self-discipline is an essential life skill to possess. It is self-control that will enable you to overcome tempting situations in your life and help you to remain on the right path when you are faced with a tough situation. Without self-control, it is hard even to achieve even the easiest task. This is because self-control is instrumental in keeping you composed and work towards your goal. It is self-control that will help you remain focused and not wander and be caught in the confusion that would arise when you follow people blindly.

Having self-control means that you are in control of your emotions and likings, particularly when you are faced with a tough situation. It is the ability to overcome your impulses for the sake of achieving your long-term goals. This implies that you will not be controlled by immediate impulses, but you will take charge of your emotions and avoid doing things that might bring regret in the future. For example, you could have purposed to eat healthily, but are tempted to have that delicious chocolate. If you don't have self-control, you will give in to temptation and take that chocolate and eventually ruin your goal of eating healthy.

Practicing self-control and willpower in difficult situations will cause you to experience great success and achievements in the long run.

Lack of self-discipline can lead to lifelong and life-damaging effects. Man is different from animals because he can impart some degrees of restraint when interacting with fellow humans. If you fail to exercise self-discipline, there might not be a difference between you and the beast. For instance, when a leopard is out there hunting, either he will be successful or not, he has no consideration for the prey, nor does it feel remorse afterward.

Human beings are made in a way that they must live on the framework set up by society. They must coexist with each other. Therefore, it is important for every person to exercise restraint dealings with others. For you to live in a congenial environment, it is necessary to control your actions towards others. However, when you lack control of yourself, there will emerge friction that would arise especially because people possess different personalities and wishes in life. When you deliberately do wrong acts towards others, you are not different from a beast. The idea of self-discipline should be brought out to depict from temptations that would lead to adverse consequences.

For you to have a more structured life and joyful life, you need to have self-control. Imagine what the world would be if every person gave in to his desires and emotions. People will not have control over any aspect of their life.

Self-control is an essential aspect of your personal growth. When you were a baby, you knew very little, but as you grow up, you become cleverer in that more was learned, although you didn't know the difference between good and wrong. However, when you were no longer a toddler, and growing up you know what is right and left through self-control. Therefore, a person can gain self-control as he matures and through exercising discipline and ensuring your emotions are in check.

Self-control is essential in all areas of your life. Be it in your relationships, while at school, in your career or while enjoying yourself with your peers. Having the ability to control yourself is probably the most important trait you will ever possess. Self-discipline is important in promoting patience within yourself. Through self-control, you can restrain some actions and ultimately increasing your ability to tolerate tough or unpleasant situations. You will experience moments of self-control when you get a hold of your emotions and try to make a change in your emotions, to positive.

When you exercise self-control, you will have increased self-esteem, and other people will see you as a person who is disciplined and in full control of your emotions and actions. The funny thing with humans is that it is easy to be controlled by others as compared to having self-control because self-control requires a lot of determination.

We have all seen what self-control is and some of its benefits, but how do we master it? Have a look below:

Methods to Master Self-Control

Having known how important self-control is in your life, it would be better to learn some of the methods you can use to master self-control. Read on and get enlightened.

Have Ways to Manage Stress

Nothing is overwhelming like going through episodes of stress. Therefore, learning how to control and manage stress will save a great deal. You can stop and take a few deep breaths to help slow your heart rate as this will put you in a relaxation mood easily. Be sure to do exercises always, take a healthy diet and have enough sleep. This will help you improve focus and your health in general. When you are experiencing low blood sugar, and you don't have enough sleep, you are likely to make poor decisions. Having regular exercises will enable you to have enough sleep and enables you to have discipline in your diet.

When you have healthy ways to manage stress, you will have enough energy to continue working, and life can feel fulfilling.

Exercise Meditation

Did you know that you can meditate your way to more self-control? When you meditate, you will have self-control skills in various areas that include the management of stress, attention, focus, and impulse control. Those people who have a tendency of meditating regularly, which develops strong willpower.

Stay Healthy

It is easy to give in to temptations when at your weakest point than when you are strong and healthy. When you are unhealthy, it may be easy for your minds to lack self-control. For instance, it may be hard for you to go to the gym and do workouts when you are having bad health. You can attain good health by eating healthy and exercising regularly. When you are unwell, the body will react in negative ways because your reserves are drained and there is not enough energy for the brain. Most arguments at home and any other places happen when people are either tired or hungry. It is easy to know someone who did not sleep enough during the night by looking at how they behave in the morning. A person who did not sleep enough will be easily upset while the one who rested well during the night will be happy and jovial.

Therefore, eating healthy and having enough sleep is essential in ensuring you have a healthy life and eventually a more controlled life.

Avoid Temptations

Human beings are not automatically wired to resist temptation. Most people resist temptation by avoiding it. Training yourself self-control by practicing repeatedly may not automatically lead to improved self-control generally. Therefore, there is no need to beat yourself up when you don't have self-control because we are not automatically wired to it. If we are not wired to self-control, how come we have disciplined people? Most people attain self-discipline by avoiding temptation, and through this, they build self-control effortlessly. You should not struggle to resist temptation but rather avoid/remove temptation.

Set yourself for growth by controlling yourself and what surrounds you by avoiding temptations. This will help you to easily make decisions automatically and reinforce yourself so that you can prioritize the decisions that are more important to you.

Avoid Self-Criticism

Having a habit of self-criticism affects self-control negatively. When you view your setbacks as an indication that you are hopeless will mess a lot of things. This is because your primary goal will be to soothe yourself instead of learning from your experiences. This might, unfortunately, lead to bad habits such as drinking alcohol, eating junk food and being addicted to the internet.

If you find yourself criticizing yourself, exercise self-acceptance instead. This will help you be more compassionate and more productive in achieving what you have purposed to do.

Chapter 6:
How to Break Bad Habits (The Right Way)

Change of any kind is very hard for us to accept and embrace. This is because we are creatures of habit. Most of our day to day activities can be categorized into several replicable habits, that we have developed through genetic predisposition and prior experience combination.

Most of our habits are harmless and are designed to enable us to become more efficient and exist comfortably in society. This includes things like going to the gym, brushing our teeth or browsing through social media regularly so that we can stay up to date. However, some psychologically complex habits are designed to protect we, like when dealing with traumatic situations through humor, staying away from a strong romantic relationship to avoid going through hurt and staying in the same unfulfilling job instead of taking responsibility and take risks.

When we maintain these habits to protect ourselves from failure, discomfort or pain, there is something wrong. Although these habits serve a role in our lives by helping you stay grounded when faced with moments of uncertainty, however over time, they impede mental anxiety and prevent growth. Your thoughts do not only affect your emotions, but they also influence the way you behave. When you have positive thoughts, you will feel better, and your performance will be awesome. On the other hand, when you think negative, you will feel despair, and this will affect your feelings and behavior.

It is normal for you to experience unrealistic, unhelpful and exaggerated negative thoughts at a time in life. When you allow cynicism to become your habit, it will limit your capabilities. It doesn't matter how experienced or talented you are; if you can't control your minds, it will be impossible to achieve great things.

Therefore, the sports psychologists help people looking towards being Olympians and athletes to eliminate the harmful self-talk that would otherwise interfere with their performance. However, not only athletes can experience benefit when they change their mindset, you can as well reap benefits when you start thinking positively. When you discover the habits that deny you of your mental capabilities is the first step towards healing your mindset. Below are some of the bad habits that can sabotage your growth:

Making Excuses

I usually tell my team that the moment you start making excuses is the moment you start failing. Blaming other individuals or circumstances for your lack of success or as the reasoning for your bad behavior derails your personal growth. Do you find yourself uttering things like," My job is weighing me down," or " All this paperwork is making it hard for me to properly do my work"? - This will impact on your performance. Refrain from a habit of making excuses and focus on things that are strongest instead of the things that you are weak. When you focus on what is positive, it will be easier for you concentrate towards achieving your goals.

You Have Negative Predictions

When you predict negatively about your future, you may just get negative results. If you go to the stage to make a performance with thoughts that you are going to mess up everything, you will not have a good focus, and you may end up forgetting your performance. Our minds tend to do what we tell them to do so being positive might make your minds sharper and free from distractions.

Seeking Approval

You should not make it your primary goal to seek approval from others because sometimes you may get discouraged. When you focus on the other person's approval, you might get in your way of doing better. For instance, let's say you are headed for an interview and in your mind, you are mostly thinking about how the interviewer would perceive your answers. This could mess you up and could make you stumble over words during the interview. Although it is important to gauge your audience's reaction towards your presentation, don't take a lot of time thinking about how they would react, but instead, focus more on your presentation.

Having Self-Doubt

One major thing that can kill your dreams is insecurity. If you walk to the gym thinking that it is impossible to gain muscles or lose weight, it is likely that you will give up before attaining your goals. When you have self-rejection, it will be hard for you to put the required effort towards achieving your goals.

Putting Yourself Down or Despising Yourself

It is difficult to gain self-discipline in any area of your life when you are telling yourself the opposite of what you want to achieve. When I was starting exercises, I could always see myself as a weak person who could not achieve building any muscles. What could happen is I was not zealous about my bodybuilding because I was always putting myself down. Until when I changed that perception about myself, that is when I started achieving my goals.

Second-Guessing Your Choices

Although sometimes it may appear okay to reflect on your past in order to make a more informed decision, second-guessing on every choice you have made could ruin your performance. When you make choices believe in them and put all the effort towards realizing them. When you start doubting, you will not have the courage to fight any challenges that you would face in the process.

Strategies on How to Break from Bad Habits

Bad habits are practices that deter you from attaining your long-term goals. It can be that you have been a chain smoker, or you are addicted to the screen most of the day that you have no time to work on your goals. To break from bad habits is not easy, especially if they bring some enjoyment to you. Below are some of the strategies to break bad habits:

Have A Reason Why You Want to Break from That Habit

For you to succeed in breaking a habit, it is paramount that you have a strong reason as to why you want to break from that habit. Note down all the reason. This will help you feel motivated. Note the harmful effects that you will experience when you continue holding to your bad behavior. For instance, if you have been too lazy to go to the gym, remind yourself of the importance of going to the gym and do workouts. Also, remind yourself what you will lose if you continue sitting on your couch and not exercising. Look at the effects of obesity on your health and how it affects your daily life. Through this, you will be having the motivation required to break from that harmful habit.

Find A Replacement with What You Want Rather

Our brains cannot remain a vacuum. If you want to be free from a bad habit, you need to give your brains a new way to move to. Set a new direction for your brains. For instance, if you want to break from screen addiction, you can use that time when you used to watch with exercise, reading or meditation. You can also minimize your free time by working more on that project you are dreaming of.

Don't Depend on Willpower

Let's be practical here.

Breaking bad habits is difficult, and willpower seems to get on the way for most people. Willpower determines whether you will push through to success or go back to your old habits. So, the secret here is to avoid willpower as you possibly can.

There is an intriguing urge to go back to our old ways on every decision we have purposed to take, and when we try to flex our willpower our "willpower tank" is drained. When the willpower is drained, you have nothing left, and you may be vulnerable to fall back to your former habits.

The secret is avoiding that difficult decision by creating a new habit. For instance, maybe you have decided to wake up early and start working. Knowing how hard it is to wake up at 4:00 a.m., you may need to make the following steps:

- Go to bed earlier
- Put your alarm out of reach while on the bed so that for you to snooze the alarm or switch it off, you will need to wake up

- Choose the clothes you will wear the night before
- Pack water or anything you may need the night before and put them a place where you can easily access them in the morning.

Although there is still some willpower involved, having avoided your willpower to make certain decisions, would help you to be successful.

Analyze the Habit

One of the ways to defeat an enemy is by knowing the tricks and his action plan. When it comes to getting rid of your bad habit, it is no different. Know where, when, why and how you are most affected by your habit. How often do you engage in it? It is paramount to understand your behavior if you desire to alter it. You can make a journal of your habits for a week or a specific duration of time. Study the patterns as this will provide the foundation upon which to change your habits.

Have A Plan and Execute Your Progress

Once you have identified the habit that you want to break, find and focus on the solution. Visualize how success is all about and how you will reach there. Going out for bigger goals might work for some people but starting small and going bit by bit towards achieving your bigger goal might be the best approach. No matter what your determination is, set a timeframe as your goal for when you ought to have completely got free from that habit. Divide your goals into milestones and track your progress as you move forward.

Employ Consistency

A substantial time is required for any habit to have roots in us and solidify in our brains, and so getting rid of it from our brains and learn other habits will also require time. The trick is to remain exercising your new habit. The more you exercise the new habit; it will make it easier for your brain to get used to it. Your brain will lay a foundation upon which you will develop your new habit fully.

For instance, when you are aiming at losing 15 pounds, you will need to go to the gym 4-5 times a week instead of exercising once per week. You will need to embrace consistency because your minds need to adopt and align towards your new direction.

Stop Exercising Bad Habits

Once you have identified a bad habit that is ruining your success and achievements, you should stop doing it. Anything that is not helping you towards realizing your goals should be starved. For instance, once you know that bad company is holding you back from breaking the habit of smoking, you should dissociate yourself from them. Once you have disconnected yourself from bad company, you will find it easy to break bad habits.

Chapter 7:
How to Force Productivity Out of Yourself

Is laziness preventing you from achieving your dreams? Do you have the feeling that your laziness is slowly destroying your life? This is like having a bloodsucking leech that secretly feeds on your leg. Life may seem okay but until you realize that you this parasite feeding you off your progress. For some people, even after realizing that laziness is getting their best of them, they don't do anything to change that. They only shrug their shoulders and allow this "parasite" to continue impacting on their life, progress, and goals. They think that they have a lot of time to change their situation, but what they miss to know is that any moment that goes is an opportunity lost. An opportunity to get rid of laziness and gives themselves a second chance for redemption.

When you choose to walk the path of laziness, you are choosing the easy path where there is no resistance. It is true that the path will bring you pleasure, but that relaxation is both futile and short-lived. In the end, the pleasure will transform into horrible pain the moment you discover that you have ruined your life. The pleasure that seems so good for a short time will turn into lifelong regrets when you realize that you lack enough time or ability to achieve your most desired goals. And as simple as that, once a promising life, turns into a life of suffering and regrets.

What is Laziness?

Laziness is a habit learned over time where we persistently and consistently resist effort in preference of a strong desire to be idle. It is a passive habit and state-of-mind we are not attentive both in our physical and mental. Some things need to be done, but we not be motivated to get them done. Therefore, we don't take proactive steps towards the direction of our goals but rather choose an easy path, where the pleasure we shall have now exceeds the benefits we may wish to get in the future. To better understand laziness, let us look if the difference between procrastination and laziness?

Having said that laziness is as a result of passive behavior, where we tend to resist effort. Procrastination is a bit different in that it is not passive but instead hesitant. This is a reluctant habit that we use to avoid acting. Procrastination is a way of defense against difficulties, potential failure, obstacles, setbacks, and criticism. When procrastinating, we are bound to have guilt. This is because we are willing to act, but we hesitate, and ultimately, we feel miserable.

On the other hand, laziness is not always attached to guilt. It is a careless behavior where one finds comfort in not doing nothing. One is not bothered to act on something strenuous or hard or can't afford to exhaust mental energies on a given task. It becomes easier to indulge in the short-lived pleasure instead of enduring pain while doing something beneficial.

Why Do You Succumb to Laziness?

We all at times succumb to laziness. However, for some people laziness is not a one-time occurrence; it is their everyday behavior. It is a regular behavior that lures us into a false sense of comfort. It may seem sometimes easy to give in to laziness, but when you look at its effects, in the long run, you better desist from it.

There are several reasons that could be making you succumb to laziness. Maybe you are feeling tired, and you use that as an escape so that you can recharge. It may seem okay because our bodies need rest but remember not to confuse rest and laziness. We take rest so that we can recuperate in doing work and putting our effort towards a task while being lazy, we simply ignore a task and use laziness to ignorance.

When you are tired and are feeling somehow bored or uninspired, it may be that you need mental awakening to remain focused and motivated. You can try challenging yourself using new ways or have creative ways to inspire yourself to get going.

You can also become a victim of laziness when you are overwhelmed. In this case, laziness is acting as a defensive mechanism the same way procrastination does. However, here you don't care. You are at a point where you care less about the outcomes, and laziness seems to be the best alternative.

It may also be that you are lazy because you are experiencing hurt or worried to face a situation or something. When you reach a point where you don't give a damn, you choose to involve yourself in laziness without feeling guilt or experiencing shame.

For you to experience the success that you so much desire, you must resist the urge to be lazy. Have a look at the following strategies that will help you defeat laziness:

How to Progress Your Goals or Life When You're Lazy and Not Be Motivated?

If you have reached a point where you are fed up with laziness, and are in search for ways to change, pay much attention to this section. You are losing out on many good things by continuing being lazy. Read on and get enlightened with the following steps:

Step 1: Find the Reason You Are Always Lazy

Like in any other solution finding venture, your first step should be to find the reason you are falling victim for laziness. Pause for a moment and look at all the reasons that make you lazy. You can do this by asking yourself the following questions:

- What is the exact reason that makes you embrace laziness?
- Are you simply uninspired, bored, just overwhelmed or fatigued?
- What are afraid of or avoiding?
- Are you afraid to act or you're using laziness as an avoidance mechanism?

When you understand why you are lazy will help you a lot in building an action plan to overcome laziness. For example, if your laziness is a result of being bored, you will find ways to restrict yourself from being bored. If it is out of fear that you become lazy, you must find better ways to understand your fears.

Step 2: Explore the Long-Term Effects of Laziness

Now that you have discovered the reasons that make you lazy, now it is time to explore the long-term effects of your laziness. You have already seen how laziness lures you with the short-term benefits and pleasures which is well and good. We all fall victim of this sometimes; however, in the long-run, that short-term pleasure may lead to a lot of pain when we start regretting on the opportunities that we missed.

The main reason we find ourselves "finding refuge" in laziness is that there is the absence of enough urgency or pain to make us do the opposite. We have a short-term view of life and base our decisions on what will make you feel good now. And in such situations, laziness presents itself as the best alternative. It provides us with short moments of pleasure without experiencing guilt or pain.

Therefore, for you to break the cycle of laziness, try and refocus yourself. You must shift on your focus and attention. This means that instead of concentrating on the short-term pleasure that comes with laziness, you should focus on the long-term effects that will come if you continue to fall victim of laziness. Laziness eats us slowly by slowly as time goes by and its consequences may not be seen now, but in the long run, its effects will be far-reaching.

When you are tempted to give in to laziness, ask yourself:

- How does laziness hurt you?
- What are you potentially missing as a result of laziness?
- What are the long-term results if you continue giving in to laziness?

When you regularly give in to laziness, you are strengthening it. Sadly, laziness will lead to negative consequences due to missed opportunities.

Step 3: Put in Place Achievable and Challenging Targets

One mistake that people make when setting goals is to set goals that are so much beyond their abilities. When they are overwhelmed by those goals, they might use laziness as an escape mechanism. Therefore, when setting your goals, make sure they are achievable but at the same time challenging. Keep them challenging enough to maintain your stimulation and interest. Pursuing a much easier goal can also lead to boredom, which is a major trigger of laziness. People who embrace a habit of laziness have no clear and concise goals. And for the few who have, they are not inspired by their goals to wake up in the morning with passion and energy.

The secret to getting rid of laziness is to have a clear picture of what you are looking for. Asking yourself the following questions might help:

- What do you dream of achieving?
- What goals stimulates or inspires you daily?
- What projects are passionate about?
- Why are you achieving those goals?
- What goals are achievable but challenging?
- Why must you achieve these goals?

Asking yourself these questions will help you in setting your goals. However, this is not enough. A lot of people set goals and do nothing towards achieving them. For you not to fall into this class, you must be specific on what is required to achieve those goals. You should know what is exactly involved in making your goals achievable. Know the routines you will need to develop and act as a foundation to attain your goals and know major tasks you would need to employ for you to hit your target.

After you have identified what is needed to achieve your goals, create stimulating tasks that offer both the challenge and excitement to you. If you set boring tasks, it is easier for you to go back to your lazy ways. Have a specific deadline within which you should achieve your tasks as this will encourage you to work more quickly. However, note that setting deadlines and priorities alone will not help you to overcome laziness completely. Ensure your tasks are engaging, fun and enjoyable.

Step 4: Take Quick Small Actions

When trying to overcome laziness, don't make the mistake of doing too much in a short period. This will cause you to be overwhelmed.

It is true that after you have laid out your goals and outlined the tasks to focus on, you may find it necessary to take immediate actions without delay. However, be sure to do this by taking small actionable steps. Concentrate on one thing at a time. Through this, you will avoid the pressure that would come in trying to achieve all your goals once but do things at the pace you are comfortable.

Ask yourself:

- What is that one thing you could do that would take you closer to your goal?
- What should you focus on primarily?

While working on your task, remind yourself:

- Making a few steps is better than not making any step at all
- After the pain you are experiencing now, you will have the pleasure

- You'll do what is necessary now for you to have what you want later

Remember even in the long-distance race; the slow and steady emerges the winner. Don't put yourself in the pressure of trying to do everything at a go. Just do something and do it consistently over time and you will see the progress. For instance, if you are targeting losing 20 pounds in your weight, don't beat yourself up when you don't realize it within one week. Have a plan and execute it consistently and before you know it, you will realize your goal. That's the only way you can achieve your goal and be happy.

Chapter 8:
The Morning Routine Fix

There is a saying that goes, "the early bird catches the worm". Have ever thought what walking up would mean for your career, your business or studies? It can bring a lot of impacts if incorporated with the right mindset. What I have learned over time is that you no need to set your alarm to wake you up very early in the morning if you are going to sit on your screen before starting your work. Having a good morning routine is about having the right mindset and doing the important things first before anybody takes your attention.

Maybe you are the kind of person who is always obligated and have so much to handle that you feel you are always running short of time. You can change all that and have a productive and organized day by exercising a good morning routine. Most successful people use morning routines as a deal breaker towards a successful and productive day.

Having a great morning routine does not revolve about who achieves more than the other; it is about giving yourself an opportunity to start the day with peace, confidence, and positivity. Starting your day well will enable you to complete your tasks as expected and deal with whatever comes your way without much pressure or stress.

Why is Having a Morning Routine Important?

Helps You Become More Productive

When you have a morning routine, it will help you tone for your day. It gives the ability to take charge of your schedules instead of schedules taking charge over you. When you begin your day well, you will be more focused on what is ahead, and manage your time well, and ultimately your productivity will increase.

Being productive does not only revolve around how much you have achieved but also the quality of willingness you are putting towards your tasks. For instance, you can end the day with eight attempted but not completed tasks, and another person does only four but fully completed tasks. The one with four fully completed tasks will feel proud than you because of the quality of work he has done. Having a well functional morning routine will mean that you will find a well-planned day minus stress.

You Will Have Both Emotional and Physical Health

It is evident that when you begin your day right by having a great morning routine, the remaining part of your day will be stress-free. You will not have pressure when in your working place which is common among most working people. When you minimize stress will be compromised, and you will be safe from diseases such as allergies, flu, colds, and other common health problems.

Again, your emotional is mostly dependent on your physical health. Again, it is hard to remain smiling when you have been caught up by tasks that need to be done. When you are late you will be overwhelmed and even frustrated. When this becomes the order of the day, you will feel like giving up because you may think it is impossible to get on track again. To avoid this, have a morning routine as it will be instrumental in giving both physical and emotional health.

You Will Be More Confident

When you go through the day completing all the tasks that you had purposed, your confidence will be boosted. Morning routine gives you confidence in that it helps you to prioritize things, manage your time and be more productive.

You Will at Peace

Imagine what goes through your mind when you see yourself as a failure each day. It can cause a lot of damage to your relationships, careers, emotions and your physical. You will always experience negative voices that will lead to distress and feel overwhelmed. You can save yourself from this by having a good morning routine that you are consistent with. It will allow you to exercise meditation, which will give you a significant way to begin your day. When you organize your day and be successful, you will be more peaceful knowing that you have achieved your day's goals. When you become consistent in fulfilling your day's tasks, your life will be peaceful generally.

For you to have a fruitful day, you must exercise some right habits.

Below is a six-morning ritual that most successful people have adopted and seen results, although they may seem difficult to practice.

Make Your Plan the Yester Night

Although this is not a morning routine, it is a habit that will play a significant role in having a fruitful morning routine. Therefore, for you to have a productive morning, have put in place plans the night before your morning. Having your things for the following day set before the morning comes is much more helpful in achieving your goals. Buy anything you feel you will need for your breakfast and write down a schedule on what you need to be accomplished the following day.

All these may sound very easy for you but believe me that by the time you arrive home after the day's work, the last thing your minds would like to think is about tomorrow's plans. You are easily tempted to get in your couch and enjoy your favorite drink, thinking that tomorrow will worry for itself.

Embrace A Habit of Waking Very Early

If you are like me, I like snoozing my alarm anytime I don't feel like waking up, but for the sake of having a successful morning, you should let this habit go. For the past two to three years I have been studying about morning routines, I have been able to learn that the most successful people wake before 6 a.m. and others even before 5am during weekdays.

I know this does not sound well to most of us, but considering the benefits that you will get, it's worth the sacrifice. The point to go with here is: successful mornings begin very early in the morning.

Begin the Day with Exercises

Although only a few people want to wake up and do exercises in the morning, it has many good things. Morning is likely the best moment to do your workouts. When you begin the day with exercise, it will not be easy for you to put it off. I came to see morning exercises as an important component of our life when I realized that even the busiest people in the world find time to exercise in the morning. I came to think if some of the prominent CEOs can find time for this what of me? A good example is the former president of USA Barack Obama, begins his day with early exercises. Despite him being too busy than most of us, he finds time to exercise. I concluded it must be a very important habit to include in our daily lives.

Handle Your Most Important Projects

I usually use my morning hours to handle some of my high-priority work because at that time there are few interruptions. It also allows me to give it more attention because before my attention shifts to other things. Usually, your wife, children, and even your boss and colleagues can get your attention during the day and so by having a morning routine will ensure you deal with your most challenging tasks before they do.

When I started on business, I used to get distracted by meetings and other interruptions that I could not manage to do anything substantial. I decided to handle my personal projects very early in the morning and concentrate on them. Having that very few visitors could visit before 7 a.m., I managed to focus and realized that I now achieved more.

Handle Other Side Projects

Most of us have a side project that we wish we could work on, but do you find time for it? It is easy to skip your side hustles, after you have been through a busy day, feeling tired and exhausted. Most of the time the only thing on your mind is what you will have for dinner and sleep. For this reason, it is advisable to use some time in the morning before engaging in your day's work for your side project. In fact, most successful people do this.

I personally use my morning hours to prepare a religious book before going for my business. Through this, I can peruse and read through many articles and write some pages before going for my day's work. By creating time in the morning and write, and do it consistently, I can commit to its success.

Just like me, you should not forgo your personal projects; rather, you should use your mornings to do it before engaging in your daily activities.

Meditate

Our daily activities can make it difficult for us to have moments where we are free. It may be that your day is filled with engagements and always going up and down in the morning, that you are unable to do meditation.

However, regardless of how busy you are in the morning, find time to do meditation. Practice a habit of having a quiet moment when starting your day daily. You can spend that moment praying, meditating, reflect on your vision concerning the future, reflect on the positive things that you have gone through – or whatever you prefer. Having that short time quiet time offers you an excellent mindset to face your day.

Chapter 9:
Become More Productive in Less Time

Is there is an area of your life that needs self-discipline; it is in managing your time. Being able to manage your time is so instrumental in determining the kind of life you will live. It is hard to manage time, but by managing yourself, you will discover that your time is well spent.

Managing time involves managing your life rather than dealing with issues and circumstances. Time is perishable; it cannot be saved. Time is irreplaceable; nothing else can replace it. Time is irretrievable; once it is gone or wasted, you can never get it back. Finally, time is indispensable, especially for the accomplishment of any kind. All achievement, all results, all success requires time.

Now that it is evident that it is impossible to create time, the trick is to manage it in a different way. You can do this by spending your time in areas of your life where you prioritize more, instead of areas that have little or no value to you. This is the key to your achievement and the need to fully exercise self-discipline.

Time management involves having what it takes to choose the order of your events. By exercising self-discipline in how you spend your time, you will know what should happen first, followed by what and even what should be removed from your to-do list. This is a choice that you should make freely.

One of the habits that holds a lot of people back from being able to manage their life and ultimately time is procrastination. Procrastination has denied most people their great success and achievements. For you to overcome procrastination, you will need to exercise much self-discipline. Procrastination is a life snatcher. It steals all your dreams making you lose who you were meant to be.

There are some things in life that are more important than others. The challenge that a lot of people face is the most valuable things that we have committed ourselves to are hard and challenging. Most of the things that we find easy and enjoyable to do are more and have no meaningful impact on life. To know the importance of anything has in your life, look at the amount of time you have invested in it. It is common for people to pay attention and prioritize the one thing that they value most. For instance, I value exercise a lot, so part of my priorities when planning my day is ensuring I commit myself to at least 1 hour for workouts daily. To my friends who do not value exercise, that is crazy. By just looking at how someone spends time, you can know what he/she values.

The key to time management is having the discipline to put in place clear priorities and stick to them. Self-discipline is what will allow you to resist the habit of watching television when for instance you should be studying. How you spend your time is like your investment. Imagine you would be keen investing those 1 million dollars knowing that you will not get other money? You will apply all your knowledge to ensure that you get the best out of it. It's the same way you should do with your time to get the best return out of it.

We waste time through procrastination when we don't have self-discipline. You can find yourself wasting your valuable time on tasks that have little value and forego the one with high returns without realizing that what you do frequently becomes your habit. Most people have therefore developed a habit of procrastination, engaging in tasks that have no spoils and leaving the most important tasks unattended.

When developing discipline towards time management, you should ask yourself; what are the consequences if I don't finish this task or not? If you find that there will be serious effects when you don't complete it, them allocate it time to be completed and vice versa.

To better understand time management, have a look at the following tips:

Wake Up Early

Almost all successful people that I have met have one thing in common: they wake up early so that they can make better use of the day. By this, they can have to prepare themselves to face the day. You can use the morning before you go to work to pray, meditate or do anything that may work for you before starting official duties. For those of you who like exercises like me, it will save a big deal.

Have A Schedule for Your Day's Goals?

By planning your daily work, you will be able to know what the day awaits you and make more efforts towards your goals. For you to be successful, you should realize the line between the high priority and urgent matters and those that can wait. This will help you to balance them during the day and leave those that are not urgent.

For my case, I work on the most important issues in the morning before looking at the emails and messages that have the potential to derail your progress. By breaking your tasks this way, you are to work towards your progress easily.

Some people advise that you split your time into two: focus time and buffer time. Focus time is when you should involve yourself in your main projects, whereas buffer time is for your small tasks. This can also help because you are able to give full concentration on your priority projects.

Avoid Multitasking

Are you serious? Yes, you heard me right. Multitasking might seem to be working towards your benefit, but in actual sense, it may be derailing you. The point here is when you do things at a slow pace you will put in all the necessary attention to all details and ultimately you will be more efficient and see more results. On the contrary, trying to accomplish a lot in a short period will make you overwhelmed leading to unnecessary stress.

Most of the people who prefer multitasking, miss having things done in the right manner. People tend to start so many things, but none of them are completed in the right manner. Instead of this, slow down a bit and focus fully on one goal at a time. By the time you are done, you will realize that no correction is required. This way you will move to your next project being proud that your former task is complete.

Create Deadlines for Your Goals

When you have set goals for yourself with definite deadlines, it will be easy to focus on their achievement. Lack of setting deadlines will make you think that you have a lot of time. Which is not always true because it can lead to procrastination.

Apart from the deadline that the client has given you, create your own short goals so that you will remain motivated to hit your target on time. If your deadline looks far away, you can break it into bits that you can achieve along the way. Focus on your small task at a time, and if you feel you are procrastinating, break it further to even smaller bits. Break them into smaller tasks to a point where it is hard to convince yourself that they are unattainable.

This is a trick used by many to avoid putting the whole project on hold until when the deadline is almost. You can also motivate yourself when you achieve your small projects. Find what motivates you and reward yourself.

Don't Be Hesitant in Acting

The mistake that all of us make at times is delaying taking actions when things arise. However, for you to save time and achieve more, have a habit of dealing with things as soon as they happen instead of waiting until when it is too late. Big problems always originate from small problems when left unattended for a long time. Therefore, don't make the mistake of ignoring a small matter when it arises before you may prevent the buildup of bigger issues that at the end will require more time to resolve.

Small issues that come in your way can be a hindrance to your progress when not solved. Always finish what you have started and when there arise some issues don't put them aside that you will deal with them later. For instance, maybe you are dealing with a project and realize there is something you have forgotten to include, don't tell yourself that you will come to it later. Resolve that issue and then move forward.

Avoid All Distractions

Are you the kind of person who usually gets distracted by phone or internet when working on your project? You can save yourself from that distraction by staying away from your phone and disable your computer notifications until when done with your work.

It is possible to get distracted by internal and external factors and sometimes you may be unintentionally using your distractors to escape from playing your role. It is paramount you understand what your distractors are and learn on ways you can avoid them. For instance, I usually turn off my phone and snooze all notifications during the time I am writing my project. This way I can stay focused for the time I have dedicated to my work. If you are working from an office, you can tell your secretary not to allow anyone in until when through. This will ensure your time is well spent by giving full attention to your goals.

Learn the Art of Saying NO

"NO" is a two-letter word but can determine whether you will be successful or not. Have you ever been in a situation where you feel that saying NO could have helped? I have many times. One day I was invited to a meeting that I felt I should not go. However, because now, I had not learned to say NO, I went for the sake of appeasing them. I was so frustrated in the meeting that when I look back today, I feel sorry for myself that I wasted my whole day instead of doing something productive. You may find yourself in a meeting and you are offered something that you don't like, but because of your inability to say no, you spend a lot of time trying to refuse the offer without offending anyone.

Again, as much as saying "No" is important, the same way saying "YES" is paramount for your success.

Delegate Some Duties

One is better than one. Sometimes you will be forced to delegate some of your projects as a way of time management. However, this should be done more carefully because it is paramount to delegate your work to the most qualified persons. When you have a great team, it will be easier for you to accomplish more within a short duration of time.

Chapter 10:
Why You Procrastinate in Explained in 15 Minutes

Are you not frustrated when there is something to be done, but you can't do or have the motivation to do it? Most people procrastinate at a point in their life, however for some people it has become a habit to procrastinate on anything that needs to be done. But have you ever asked yourself what makes you procrastinate and not do the things that are more important but instead do things that have the least importance? It is really tempting to watch your favorite movie instead of doing that assignment.

The major reason that makes it challenging to deal with procrastination is, because each person has a different reason for procrastinating. Each person has several reasons for procrastinating on different things. Excuses that procrastinators give are so similar. First, they always think that they will have time to do a task. Although this is not always true because there is a habit of postponing and when the time they had postponed to comes, they will still give the same excuse. Sometimes they will claim they are held up, and so they cannot commit to doing a task. They know they need to exercise, but they will claim they can't get time for it now.

For you to stop procrastinating and get things done immediately, you must know the reasons why you are procrastinating. Through this, you will be able to handle it and even eliminate this habit.

Without going further, check the following reasons as to why you procrastinate:

You Are Afraid of The Unknown

Most of us fear stepping out to get things done because we are not sure what the results would be. For instance, you may be having a health concern that you are afraid that when you go to the hospital and get the problem diagnosed, the results may be traumatizing. So, you prefer to stay with your condition hoping that it will just go away on its own. Sometimes you are afraid that by taking that step, some truths that you are not willing to bear will come to light.

I disagree with the saying that says that "what you don't know won't hurt you". This is because when you assume a problem it will get worse and you will be too late when you realize that.

When you allow misconception to control your mind, it will influence the way you think, and you won't be able to act even when you know you are headed the wrong direction. You will go on living in misconception, particularly if it lines with what you believe. You will in misconception tell yourself that this thing will pass away on its own with time or none of my family members has gone through this before, and so I am fine.

But think about this what if for instance you are talking about a disease like cancer that can be handled in its early stages? Would it be better to act early than wait?

Fear to Make A Mistake

Most people procrastinate because they think that in stepping out and do something, if they fail, they will expose themselves. They believe in perfection. Do you find yourself failing to do things because you fear making mistakes? It is so dangerous as it can lead to procrastination.

Anything that you find yourself doing is a product of your mindset. For you to succeed in any area of your life, be it in athletics, arts or even music, your minds must be set for success. You can either have a "fixed mindset" or a "growth mindset". When you possess a "fixed mindset", you tend to believe that your abilities are limited and it's probable that you will not experience growth. On the other hand, those with a ``growth mindset" believe that they are limitless and can develop and prosper by working hard. They believe that they have unlimited abilities and can step out without concentrating on failure.

When you fear making mistakes, you will only do things that you believe are in line with your perfection and avoid tasks that would require you to put a little more effort to accomplish. Although some may argue that this is a good trait, it is so harmful to you and a great enemy of progress.

Fear of Success

Yes!! Some of the reasons that you procrastinate are because you fear the pressure that comes with succeeding. Sometimes you may feel that when you succeed people will expect more from you going forward. Or that when you succeed, you will be known by many people and maybe you prefer a private life.

Most often, this kind of procrastination happens to people who have low self-esteem, and so their worth is mostly tied to their achievements. You may find yourself challenging yourself on how much you should put up so that you can be perfect. And so, any achievement will mean more expectations to your minds.

Over time this may lead to you losing identity and sometimes you don't feel like you own your success. This will ultimately lead to procrastination as a way of avoiding the pressure of always trying to be better.

Thinking That You Can Do It Later

Do you get telling yourself that you will do a certain task later? If you said yes, watch out because you may be a victim of procrastination. This is a lie that shows that in the time to come you will have a perfect opportunity to carry out your task.

It may be that you wanted to do exercises in the morning before going to work. But your minds tell you that the best time to do it is in the evening after finishing your duties. This may sound like good advice in the morning, but the reality is when evening comes, you may be tired and hitting the gym may be difficult.

What you may not know is that your mind is trying to give solace now at the expense of your goals and dreams. Again, your mind changes with time and whatever you have decided you will do later, or date may be subject to the state of mind that you will be when that time comes.

Working on Easier Tasks

This is common to most people. It is easier for you to browse through Facebook and emails rather than settle on that research project. How many times have you found yourself talking with your colleague instead of working?

Think of the many easier tasks that you have put in place when you don't feel like dealing with real issues. Although these tasks tend to make you busy and engaged, it is just a form of procrastination you've created. The reason why you find yourself engaging in easier tasks is that you can finish them quickly and have an instant sense of fulfillment. The more challenging and harder a task is, the more time you will need to do, and chances are you may engage in procrastination and avoid them. This is because you may see the benefit as being so far.

Lack of Motivation

Most of the time I have people say that I don't like what I am doing. If you have a habit of doing only things that you feel motivated to do, there are high chances that you procrastinate a lot. This is because most of the things that you may find on your to-do list may not motivate you. For instance, waking at 5.00 a.m. and have a walk before going to your work is not an easy thing and you will need self-discipline to achieve that.

Your attitude towards a task could be working against you achieving your goals. What do you think when the idea of stepping out and do something strikes you? If you feel that laziness strikes when you are supposed to do something, then your attitude is coming in the way of your success. You should have ways to tackle that if you are to succeed. Imagine if you depend on what you feel so that you could do anything? Most things would remain undone because our minds would easily avoid challenging tasks.

Lack of Knowledge to Complete A Task

When you don't have the necessary skills to start and complete a task, you are most likely to procrastinate on it. For instance, if you are given a task to write a book and you don't have the skills required to handle it, it is probable that you might avoid that task.

Due to human nature, you may not even have the courage to inquire, and so the only option for you will be to procrastinate. Your mind will be inclined to avoid the task instead of going out and learning the skills to do that task. At some point, I was a victim of this in my life especially when with my friends. I preferred not to do something that I was unsure of instead of doing it the wrong way and appear dumb to them. Here you will use procrastination as a defense against being mocked when you lack the required skills to do a certain task.

Lack of Interest

When you lack interest in doing a certain task, there are high chances that you will start procrastinating. All of us, on some occasions, lack interest in things that we are supposed to do, but this should not automatically imply that you stop doing that thing.

When you don't have an interest in your goals, it is easy to get distracted with other things that have little benefits that may appear more appealing to you now. For example, you may have an assignment that you are supposed to do, but because you don't have an interest, you may start playing games or browsing the internet. This will lead to procrastination, and before you discover it, you will have wasted a lot of time. You can avoid this kind of procrastination by forcing yourself in activities that you are not interested if they are supposed to be done.

You Are Easily Distracted

Are easily distracted by text messages, social media, Skype, phone, emails, etc.? Distraction is affecting the productivity of employees more than can you imagine. These distractions eat into your time making you procrastinate on doing your most important duties. That time when you are browsing the internet or make an unrelated phone call, you could use it to make your goals a reality.

It is easy for you to give in to distractions depending on the kind of task you are dealing with. When you are doing a challenging or difficult task, and for instance, a message from your friend appears on the screen, you will be tempted to look at the message to avoid that challenging task. Therefore, keeping yourself away from all distractions will help, especially if you are not disciplined enough to say no to distractions.

You Always Avoid Hard and Challenging Tasks

Sometimes we tend to avoid tasks that need a lot of effort. Some projects will also require you to give up on some habits for you to accomplish them. For instance, if you are working towards losing weight, you will be required to work extra hard and even wake up early so that you could have time for exercises. There are also some foods that you will require to stop taking like junk foods and fatty foods.

If you are not very serious about losing weight, you may use this as an excuse to procrastinate and avoid putting up with exercises. A project can be challenging in that it requires your patience for you to achieve it. Losing weight is not something that you can achieve overnight. Also, most successful business persons employed patience to reach where they are today. It is easy for you to procrastinate after realizing that it will take quite some time before you realize your goals. People like instant rewards and results. By procrastinating, you will find other simple activities to engage in instead of putting the necessary effort to achieve your goals.

Chapter 11: Over Come Procrastination Through Self-Discipline

In the immediate chapter, we have looked at what causes us to procrastinate on our goals. In this chapter, we are going to look at methods you can use to stop procrastinating. We all find ourselves in this situation: the deadline to a task is approaching, but instead of using any time we have towards achieving our goal, we find ourselves engaging in less meaningful activities like social media, playing games, browsing through the internet and checking emails. You understand you should be doing a task, but you are not in the mood to do it.

Procrastination is common to people of all classes. When procrastinating, you tend to avoid the important things you should be doing until when the deadline is too close, you are overwhelmed and wish you could have started earlier.

Some people are so much in procrastination that they tend to postpone everything in their life and always remain in the same cycle. When you have a habit of putting things off, avoiding work and only working when the task in question is not avoidable, you will never achieve anything great in life. The good thing is there is a solution if you carefully exercise the following:

Break Your Goals into Small Bits

As said in an earlier chapter, one of the major reasons that people procrastinate is because they have a huge work log that they feel overwhelmed. By breaking your project into smaller portions, you will be able to concentrate on one portion at a time. If when working on those portions that you have broken, you still procrastinate, break your project into even smaller portions. When you do this, you will not have any excuse to delay doing your project.

For instance, if you are planning to start a supply business that will cover the whole country, you can plan your business in such a way that you will start your supply in the capital city first. Later, after covering the capital city, you can go on to another town. Through this, it will be easier to concentrate on each portion of the project without being highly overwhelmed.

Have a plan on how you will progress in your project until you cover the whole country by having manageable parts of the project. Concentrate on each phase without thinking on other parts until when you are through with it, and then you can move to the next.

Have A Strong Reason Why You Must Act?

One of the main reasons that we procrastinate is because we focus on our short-term fulfillment or benefits. We tend to avoid the stress that comes with staying committed and instead enjoy the short-term pleasure that comes with it, not knowing that it may bring long term suffering by not acting. You should focus on the benefits you will get on doing that task no matter how hard or uncomfortable you may be when doing it.

If, for instance, you are aiming to lose weight. Imagine how comfortable and healthy you will feel when you have attained the weight you so much desire. If it is a business, visualize the profits you will get when you have got things going. Instead of focusing on the sacrifice that you will make to achieve your goals, visualize the product.

This will not only make you motivated but will help you to focus on the final prize or reward. When you keep your mind on the reward it will be easy for you to stop procrastinating and get things going.

Be Realistic When Setting Your Goals

When setting your goals, you must be realistic. Set in place doable and achievable goals. It is good to aim higher, but don't make the mistake of aiming what is not achievable. Be realistic in the amount of time you give yourself to complete your tasks. Setting very short deadlines than what can be possibly achieved will only lead to frustration.

Projects tend to take more time than we anticipated and so give yourself enough time to complete the project. I don't know what you think will happen when you don't have enough time to complete a task. It feels awful and overwhelming. When overwhelmed your mind may tend to tell you that the only option is to avoid doing the task because you will not succeed within the deadline you have set yourself.

If you are starting on exercises, you must start with light exercises like walking for 10-20 minutes in the morning. When you set yourself for huge tasks at the start, you may find yourself giving up before you even start. Therefore, being realistic in terms of the task and the time within which you want to accomplish a task will enable you to achieve your goals and avoid procrastinating.

Remove Distractions

When working towards stopping procrastinating, you must keep your environment from all distractions. Your environment can hinder your growth. Remove all distractions, especially the ones that you know can tempt you easily. In my case, I usually keep away from social media when working on a project because they can distract me easily.

The kind of environment that you are working on is determinant of the work you will do. Look at how your office or room is arranged. How is your desk arranged? Anything that you feel can make your attention to shift, change it. During the time that you have set to work on a task, remove all distractions. Sometimes you will be forced to switch off your phone, snooze notifications on your desktop and avoid talking to your colleagues when you should be working. Let your mind be focused on finishing your project first before engaging in any other task. Through this, you will give all your attention to the task, and you will achieve more.

Exercise Self-Forgiveness

Are you the kind of person who usually beats yourself up does to past mistakes? You better stop because that may be the reason you are always procrastinating. Saying negative things towards yourself will only lead to frustration. Saying things like "I always waste time" or " I am always a loser" is so detrimental towards your progress. Even when you have procrastinated in the past, forgive yourself so that you can be able to deal on your current task well.

Make use of your experience with procrastination to your advantage. You can do this by trying to ask yourself what caused you to procrastinate on your past project or task. Is it stress, distractions or lack of skills? What it is that you find makes you procrastinate? Find ways to address them at that moment going forward. If it is lack of skills that made you avoid tasks, you should put in place measures to learn more skills so that in the future you will not procrastinate.

Also, by forgiving yourself, you will give yourself an opportunity to refocus and handle things differently. If you find that your avoidance is due to putting wrong priorities or unrealistic goals, you will be able to come up with good plans. You will also have peace of mind and confidence that is so instrumental in your moving forward.

Stop Giving Excuses

Most of the time we are held back by excuses. Do you find yourself saying the following things? 'I will visit you once I have time", " I am not in the mood", "I wish so and so could be here, I could do this" and the like? You need to refrain from that habit if you opt to move forward and achieve your goals.

You must be realistic to yourself and realize whether they are good reasons holding you back, or it is just an excuse. We tend to use excuses when we want to avoid acting and not feel guilty. So, we hold on excuses and convince ourselves that we have a good reason for not doing what we were supposed to do. We all find it good to be in the mood when doing something, but we should not allow that to stand in our way of achievements.

Some of the things that present a lot of benefits are not motivating and so waiting until when you are in the mood may mean that you will never do them. Waking up early so that you can find time to do your side project is not an easy thing. But when you decide and do it the benefits will be so pleasing. This means you must act even when your emotions are saying otherwise.

Don't Keep Your Goals Secret

Although some people prefer keeping their goals secret. When you want to stop procrastinating, this may not apply. When you know that no one knows about your plans, it may be easy to sleep over them and not act because there is no one will put you into account when you don't achieve them. I recommend that you share your goals and dreams with someone who will hold you into account when you don't complete what you had purposed.

This can be your partner, your teacher or even your boss. Sometimes you will also need to look for a coach who will ensure that you are doing what is expected. A perfect instance is when you are working towards losing weight. You will need to have a coach who will guide you on the kind of exercises you should do. You may also need to have a nutritionist who will guide you towards achieving your goal. With all these people to monitor you, you will be forced to put all the necessary efforts so that you succeed because you know you will be ashamed in the case you fail.

Avoid Perfectionism

Do you tend to believe you are nothing when you fail, or you are something when you succeed? This is not a good mentality. This is a mentality that shows that you are either perfect or nothing. People with this mentality wait until when the situation is perfect for them to do something. They are always in search of the perfect time to begin an assignment or start a business. Waiting until you are 100% sure that what you are about to do will succeed may translate that you will not start at all. This mentality can hold you back and taking steps towards starting a project may be impossible.

Instead of this mentality, you should focus on doing your best. This means that you will work your best towards a goal.

To avoid procrastinating when planning to start a project, don't focus on finding the perfect time, perfect place or anything perfect – you may never find it, rather concentrate on better. For instance, you may never find a perfect place to start a business, but you can find a better place. Through this, you will not waste your time on where to get a perfect place, but rather use that energy towards promoting development.

Look for Role Models

Anything that you are trying to accomplish it is probable that there are people who have gone through it and succeeded. Let's say you are trying to lose fat and you are at the verge of procrastinating, finding someone who has been through it will motivate you to work harder. Connect with them and learn what secrets they used in hitting their target.

Knowing that upon putting in the necessary effort towards your goals you can achieve them will motivate you a lot. One of the reasons that people procrastinate is because they think that their situation is unique and that no one has been there before. But by moving out and seeking mentors, you will be astonished when you learn that others have been there and succeeded.

Don't Take Long to Plan – Act

One of the reasons that most people procrastinate is because they take a lot of time in the planning process. Think about how much time you have been planning to work on your diet, to stop complaining or even start that new business. Over planning can easily lead to inaction. You may strategize, plan and hypothesize, but if no action is put in place, nothing will be achieved.

It is easy for you to sit down and complain, but the question that you should ask yourself is; what are you doing to change your situation? Take actions now, and before you know it, success will be knocking your way- Stop Procrastinating!

Chapter 12:
Growth Mindset to Achieve Anything

Our mindset affects how we act and our potential for acting. People who have a mindset that can be improved through hard work, learning, improving strategies and even change of environment, have a growth mindset. They achieve more than those individuals that have a fixed mindset. People with a growth mindset are not bothered when they start small because they believe they can navigate through hard work and improved strategies and experience success.

People possess a mix of both a fixed and growth mindset – the mindset changes depending on the environment, circumstances and the type of hardships we are facing. Our mindsets can also be affected by the way we were brought up because children minds are easy to change during upbringing.

Mindset is so important because it determines what we will achieve in life. Therefore, you need to guard your mindset by having a clear view of your growth. Ask yourself, what pushes you towards growth? Is it when facing challenges? When taking risks? Or even when comfortable. By doing this, you will know how to avoid having a fixed mindset.

Many things affect our mindset, and so we need to be so careful about things that we embrace. People that have a growth mindset and exercise it more regularly can find ways to avoid old bad habits. This is because their minds are always finding solutions. With a growth mindset, you can embrace change and are open to different ideas.

Long-term thinking is so instrumental in developing self-discipline and succeeding in life. When you look at the business giants in the world, they all had a long-term plan for their business that enabled them to reach their current levels. Therefore, if you are dreaming of succeeding in life and being different from your peers, you must embrace long-term thinking. When you think long-term and have a plan to reach there, although what you do daily may not seem to show results, but slowly, you will make strides towards your goals.

Imagine when you were a child when your parents gave you a small amount of money to use on whatever that may interest you. Your only thought was to go directly to the shop and buy your favorite toy or popcorn. This is because you were more concerned with immediate satisfaction. There was no reason not to do that because you depended on your parents to give more money any time you needed.

As you grow older, it is probable that your parents would give allowances frequently, instead of giving you instant cash upon request. Your parents could give a monthly amount that he expected to take you for a specific period, let's say a month. This means that, when you wanted to do something, you first had to think, because when the money that you had been given runs out before the time to be given additional money came, you would suffer. This shows that for you to survive, you had to think long-term rather than always giving in to your short-term satisfaction.

Most people, especially those who work on monthly basis fall into the temptation of not thinking long-term. Having that they expect their salary every month, they tend to spend all their money on recurrent expenditure because they know that after 30 days or anytime, they receive their pay they will get other money. They spend all their income on their monthly needs such as paying the electricity bill, rent, buying food and even entertainment. This cycle can repeat itself month after month because it offers short-term satisfaction and is comfortable.

But that kind of strategy cannot allow you progress in life and that is why you must have in place long-term thinking.

Long-term thinking is very significant in assessing where your life is headed and in building self-discipline. No wonder you will find most employers asking the interviewees their long-term goals before hiring. This is because they know employees with long-term goals are more focused and disciplined and so working with them will lead to the success of their companies too. A long-term thinking person is goal-oriented.

One of the reasons that you find yourself obsessing on setbacks rather than focus on the long-term goals is because your minds are focused on obstacles instead of the future that you aim for.

How Long-Term Thinking Helps You Build Self-Discipline and Enhances Your Progress

When you start thinking long-term, it will be easy to build self-discipline and progress in life as opposed to thinking short-term as you will see below.

You will Move Forward Instead of Being Caught in Problems for Long

One of the reasons that we are held back is because we tend to be caught up by challenges. You should not allow what is currently taking place in your life to make you forget your long-term goals. We all pass through challenges when working on something. Many times, it is possible to think that the challenges that we are facing are an indication that we should not go ahead with our plans. However, you ought to remain focused and determined even when things get tough.

When things get tough, remind yourself that opportunities come dressed in ways that are not always pleasing. Imagine how treasure is buried in the ground and it is only the hardworking and determined that will get hold of them. Having long-term thinking will enable you to go beyond your setbacks to achieve your goals. It enables you to remain disciplined and anchored onto your goals even when things get tough.

You Don't Measure Life by Looking at Your Failures

One of the things that bring down people with short-term thinking is that they use their setbacks and failures to measure their life. But when you are thinking long-term, you will be able to avoid paying much attention to your failures because you will visualize yourself getting over them.

People with short-term thinking tend to be distracted by their setbacks so much that they forget their goals. They overstay on their failures thinking that it is over. They have a keen eye on the negative things happening in their life that they can't do anything. But, when you have long-term thinking, although you have setbacks, you will remember your long-term goals which will help you to remain focused. It is true that you will be faced by real setbacks, but through your long-term mentality, you will gather all your efforts towards your success.

You Will Remain Focused on the Final Prize

It takes self-discipline to wake up every morning and go to the gym even when you don't see quick results. With long-term thinking, you don't focus on how slow you are moving provided you are making progress. Long-term thinking also allows you to avoid taking things too seriously because you know that through patient a solution would be found.

People with short-term thinking lack a clear picture of the future they hope for. They easily give in when they are faced with hardships. Instead of concentrating on your failures, always visualize your future. We all go through tough moments in life, and although this may subject us to a lot of discomfort, they allow for essential growth for the goal before us.

You Will Be Constrained in Your Abilities

One of the differences between those people that think short-term and those that think long-term is that those that think short term is always constrained to their abilities currently whereas those that think long-term are not. For instance, when thinking short-term, you will not think beyond your financial ability, language, muscle ability and many other things. This means that when drafting their vision, it will be limited to their knowledge and abilities now. For instance, you may be dreaming of building a palatial house. When thinking short-term, your minds will argue that it is not possible to build that house because you will not be able to visualize yourself having money in the future. Through this, their dream will become weak, and eventually, their dreams will diminish.

However, when thinking long-term, you will be able to get over all limitations and step out into action. Long-term thinking allows you to believe that you will achieve any dream in your life no matter your limitations now. It allows you to navigate through and look for ways that will make you achieve by removing anything standing in the way.

People who think long-term is not easily affected by their surroundings, unlike short-term thinkers who will be affected by every detail of their surroundings. Long-term thinkers decide and stick no matter what they go through. For instance, if you have decided to start a blog, you will not allow anything to stand in your way. Even if you don't have much knowledge on the subject that you want to write, you will find the knowledge instead of doing the easier thing which is to quit or change your minds. You will make all the effort so that you could achieve.

Unfortunately, this is not what happens with short-term thinkers. They are affected by their surrounding including what their friends tell them. And if they happen to talk negative about their plans, they are likely to quit. For you to succeed in anything you have dreamed off, and not be affected by your surroundings, think long-term.

Long-term Thinking enables You to Be Patient

One fundamental principle for success is patience. All successful people have taken a lot of time to reach their destination. No huge thing can be built in a day. Imagine the time it took for brands like Amazon to grow to their present levels! It took a lot of time and patience was paramount. Without patience, it is possible to quit halfway, or at any point, you feel discouraged.

It is common for business or anything that you have started not to show results during the first stages. If you don't have long-term thinking, you can easily quit at this point. This is because your short-term thinking might show you that the project is not realistic or is unachievable. However, that is a test for your patience.

Therefore, you must learn to wait for the foundation of your project to become strong. Long-term thinking is so instrumental in ensuring that you can endure the current pain and disappointments for the sake of your long-term goals. But, when thinking short-term, you may grow impatient and even quit. Short-term thinking is after overnight success. Having that this is not always possible, it may become detrimental to your success.

When you have well laid up plans and constantly working towards your goals, patience will be a significant component of your success. You can only achieve this by thinking long-term so that you can understand why every significant growth need time.

You will develop essential characters like self-discipline and self-control when you continuously think long-term. With time you will find that you no longer struggle to do the right thing. Your mind will be set in a way that your goal and dreams are very important than your instant pleasures and satisfaction and therefore you will easily step out and act. You will see how every step you are taking is drawing you closer to your goals.

Chapter 13:
The Future is Brighter Than You Think

A motivational speaker Jim Rohm once said that " You are the average of the five people you spend the most time with". Although one can claim to have personal choices, the people that we spend time with plays a significant role in our behaviors, attitudes and beliefs. You can't argue the fact that people have a great impact on your behavior. That is why you hear things like peer pressure. Social groups are the determiner of norms and culture. It is therefore important to be keen on the impact of your associations on your behavior and success.

The Power of Associations

Anytime I think about the impact of our friends on our life, I remember a Chinese proverb that goes ``three men make a tiger". In that story, the king is asked whether he would believe when one or two citizens claim that a tiger was roaming in the city streets. The king said no. But when asked whether he would believe when three or more people repeated the same thing, interesting he said he would believe. Those around him were astonished and reminded them that it was impossible for a tiger to roam in the streets no matter how many people said so.

What do you take from that? It means that if there is many people arguing about something is true, no make how unrealistic it is, their argument might be accepted at the end. Therefore, you might find yourself agreeing to what most of your friends are saying. No matter how much you may try to remain the one with a different opinion, most of the time you might find yourself giving in. There is an attitude that is within your association, and no matter how you try to google or inquire from other sources it might not be easy to go against your associations.

The only way you can help yourself from negative impact that may arise from your association is to wisely choose who you spend most of your time with. Ask yourself, are my associations leading an interesting life, or are a negative life? Some people possess a limiting attitude and behaviors. They are dull, have negative imaginations and not interesting to stay with. You can shape your life by staying away from such people. Imagine you are planning to do exercises and change how your appearance, but your association is so negative regarding exercises. No matter how you try, it will be hard to continue exercising. They will always limit you and show how exercises will not work. This might cause you think that you are wasting your time. On the contrary, if you always hook up with people who are doing exercises, you will always feel motivated, and you will not struggle much to wake up and exercise.

Having the right association allows you to remain focused and passionate instead of going through one idea to another through life. This is because your association will be instrumental in ensuring that you are encouraged to move on no matter how tough it becomes. You will always have a strong opinion about life, and you will have a huge impact on the world. When waking up in the morning, you will be full of energy and full of enthusiasm.

Remember you are more likely to believe what three or more people say. Therefore, if many your associations have a negative attitude, you are going to be affected. If they say something is not possible which is mostly due to their limiting attitude, you are likely to join them in tune. If you spend time with people who always hang on social media, even if you aren't a fan of social media, you might be forced to change for you to fit in that group. If you spend time with people who believe their dreams are unachievable, you might as well believe that yours too are mere imaginations. Associating your life with people who focuses more on limitations and negativity, will do you more harm.

Imagine if you would surround yourself with people with the following mindsets:

People Who Always Says "I Can't Do"

The most detrimental imagination you can have towards yourself is to think that you can't achieve something. Having this kind of thought alone is so harmful that it can make you stop pursuing your goals and work on something else. It is obvious that you put your efforts on what you think you can accomplish. You should keep yourself away from people with this kind of mindset. When you are having a chat with your friends and hear them say that the reason, they are not working towards their goals is because they can't make it, know that you are associating yourself with a very dangerous character. These people will always give excuses as to why they can't make it. Associating yourself with these people might make you lose inspiration to work on your dreams.

People Who Think They Are Not Good Enough

There are some people who think that they are inferior in handling their tasks. They think that they don't have what it takes to act. Usually, this is not regarding their talents but is as a result of much negative comparison to other people. This can be so demoralizing not just to them but also to the people around them.

If you want to realize your goals, there are not the right people to hang with. Spending a lot of time with such people can make you have inferior thoughts about yourself. Surround yourself with people who have faith in themselves and believes that they can stand up and do something. Through this, you will be inspired to fight for your dreams. Sometimes the going may get tough, but when you have the right company, you will find things a bit easier.

People Who Anticipate Bad Things "What Ifs."

It is true that when indulging in something new, you will want to know the outcome. But, associating yourself with people who always think negative concerning the future is wrong. This is because those people who always are always thinking that negative things will happen, don't act. Imagine having people around you who always see something happening. You tell them you a new business idea, and the only thing that comes from their mouth is "what if it doesn't work?". It will be so challenging for you to go on with your plan.

Surrounding yourself with people who always possibility and positivity will help you to start something and succeed. It is probable that some of your goals that you have not embarked on are because you associated yourself with uninspiring people. Although many may argue that life is not certain, it could not be logic to always think negatively. Life involves taking risks. Therefore, ensure your associations are people who can inspire you to be better by taking risks. This cannot happen if you or your associates are always thinking negative.

They Are Perfectionists

Imagine staying with people who fear making mistakes, and it can be so limiting. Trying to make every detail of your life perfect can be so draining. Again, it limits someone from making any progress in life.

Staying with this kind of people might mean that you will never step out and try anything. And obviously, without trying anything, it will be impossible for you to achieve. Talk to any great achievers, and you will be astonished on how many times they tried and failed before they could succeed. No man does not make mistakes, and so no one should stop trying for fear of making mistakes. People who put much attention on being perfect, usually miss out on taking risks. They limit themselves and usually get trapped in a comfort zone.

What separates ordinary people from those whose progress is their ability to accept failure and move one. This means if you want to achieve more in life, you should check on your associations. If they happen to fear failure that it limits them from taking steps, avoid them as much as possible.

The Effects of Having Positive People Around You

The impacts you will get when you surround yourself with positive and interesting people will be astounding. People with interesting things happening in their life are so energetic and enthusiastic. When your associations are positive individuals, your attitude will be great and have a good approach towards life.

People who are working towards their dreams are risk takers and are confident that they will be successful. They have high hopes concerning their future and are willing to take any step so that they can succeed. This is the type of people you should be exposed to regularly so that you could be successful. One of the benefits that you will gain when you associate yourself with these people is that you will have a great attitude and behavior.

When these people to go forward, you will be more inspired to do the same. You will start to realize the kind of things you can do in your life. For instance, when you look at people who have been successful in the profession or business that you are planning to start, it will help you know that your dream is achievable. Understanding how they tackled the kind of hardships they faced in their journey will help you remain inspired. One of the reasons that people give up is because they think the challenges, they are facing are unique and that no one has gone through and succeeded. But, when you have people to look up to, it will be hard for you to not give up.

Different people have different ideas concerning the world. People have different passions and talents and so interacting with inspiring people will expose you to new experiences and ideas. The secret is to surround yourself with the right people.

How Do You Take Control of People in Your Life?

Know Your Goals

It is your responsibility to choose the kind of people you would like around you. You can easily do this by identifying your dreams and then hooking up with people that you believe will be instrumental in moving them forward. This can be a mentor or people that you believe offers the necessary support in terms of both attitude, behavior and skills. Having some clear deliberations for your goals will help you to have the right associations and will be important for your success.

Find Same-Minded Groups

People working towards the same purpose or target usually encounter the same problems. Therefore, engaging yourself with the same-minded people will help you remain focused and enhance personal development. In this group, people encourage each other, challenge each other and even find solutions.

If you can't find one such group around you, you can create one.

Act Like Individuals You Want to Interact With

You are likely to attract individuals that you share the same traits. If you like blogging, it is probable that you will attract other bloggers. If you are a bodybuilder, you will attract people who love workouts. This implies that after you have identified people that you want to interact with, learn their behaviors and act like them, though not blindly. For instance, in my daily travels, I have found myself easily interacting with people due to my love for sports. It has been my main conversation starter, and it also determines the kind of people I interact with.

Avoid Excuses

The time I have involved myself with positive people, I have realized they have controlled thoughts. They merely make excuses and does their best to execute their plans and achieve their goals. If you want to attract such people, you must be accountable and have control of your minds. It will be insane to think that you can live carelessly and then expect to attract inspiring people near you.

Avoid the Negative

You need to avoid the harmful thoughts and voices that distracts you from moving forward. Minimize the time you spend with people who usually criticize you. Avoid the people who lead to places you don't wish to be. Your thoughts are so important and should be guarded in any way possible.

Not just the people that you interact with physically can have an impact on your life. The magazines and books you constantly read can affect the way you read. Things that you read on the internet can also determine how your minds will think. Avoid reading content that will weigh you down. Don't allow your minds to be exposed to a lot of garbage as this will affect you badly.

Having the right people around will help you know when you are going the wrong direction, motivate you when you feel weighed down and greatly inspire you when trying to hit your target.

Eliminating Distractions from Your Environment So You Can Focus on What's Important

It is possible for you to be distracted in your work due to the many distractions available. From people to phones to the internet, so many other things can easily distract you when you ought to remain focused and productive. Distractions are so detrimental in that they make you miss deadlines and have little time to rest. Eventually, this will make you exhausted and unable to give proper attention to your work and fail to deliver your full potential.

It is easy for you to be distracted by the internet or any other distraction without knowing. Sometimes you may tell yourself - with this digital era you cannot stay away from your phone or the internet. However, before you know it, you have wasted a lot of time that you could use to do your work. If you can manage to eliminate distractions in your work, it will be easy to be focused on your goals and eventually you will achieve more.

However, for you to eliminate distractions, you should embrace the following tips:

Tips You Can Use to Eliminate Distractions

Make Your Schedule

It is easy for you to give in to distractions if you miss a proper work schedule. Having a work schedule allows you to say "NO" to too many things if not on your plan. Without a schedule, you are bound to make a lot of steps that are uncalled for and eventually find it hard to accomplish your dreams. So, the key to eliminating distractions is to have a schedule for your day and avoid deviating from it.

Have Enough Rest

One of the perfect ways to make sure that you get enough rest is to get enough sleep. Sometimes it is not easy, but it is crucial for the body. Having enough sleep gives you a better day as compared to taking coffee in the morning. A better point to start having enough sleep is to have a proper sleep schedule. Ensure you sleep enough hours, usually 7-9 hours. You can make it possible by avoiding activities that keep you awake past your scheduled sleep time. This includes avoiding things like watching tv or even overworking.

Take Healthy Diet

Always find time to eat healthily. Satisfying our cravings with donuts and junk foods is easy. However, just like our body, the brains need energy so that they can work well. Anytime you feel hungry, eat food that will give your brains energy and help you remain focused throughout the day. Through this, it will be easy to avoid being distracted.

Ensure Your Working Space is Clean

Imagine what seeing that disorganized working desk does to your mind. It causes a lot of distraction. Ensure your working space is organized so that you can minimize distractions. Whatever working space you are on, ensure it is orderly so that your work can be easily done.

Off course you can decorate your workspace with what you like but ensure it does not go overboard.

Snooze Social Notifications on Your Computer

We all know the important role that computers play in our work. However, when not carefully monitored it can be a very big source of distraction. Imagine working on your computer while social notifications are peeping on your screen? It will be very hard for you to ignore them and continue with work. Therefore, for you to remain focused on your important work, it will be better to snooze the notifications. This will enable you to put all the necessary attention to your work and achieve more.

To ensure you don't miss anything important, you can't take small breaks and check on slack, emails or any other media.

Switch the Phone Off

Looking at your phone's messages, playing games and making calls can be a big source of distraction. Therefore, switching it off and keeping away can be a great way to avoid distractions on your work.

Make People Aware You're Busy Working

Although it may seem obvious, letting people know you are working is important in eliminating distractions. The time you dedicated to work should be known to all your friends and relatives. Tell your co-workers that you don't want disturbances in a certain period for you to concentrate well. If you have a secretary, it will be easier for you because you can give her instructions not to allow visitors for the said period. You also put a sign if you feel that will keep people away. This will ensure you achieve more daily.

Exercising the above tips will be instrumental in ensuring you are not distracted. Now you can sit down and work. Also, ensure you have all the tools you may need so that you will not take much time looking for them. Avoiding distractions will ensure that you achieve more.

Chapter 14: My Number One Method to Build Self-Discipline (It Actually Works)

Self-discipline involves doing things that we don't like so that we can achieve our goals. It requires self-discipline to take the right food and do workouts. It is not easy to avoid eating chips or that donut you love so much. It needs regular practice and dedication for you to achieve it. Just like you improve each day on exercises as you practice, so you get used to eating the right food even if you don't like it.

When I wanted to lose weight, I knew I had to do something with my diet. I always felt uncomfortable, and I felt embarrassed most of the time. Concentration was becoming a problem and before I knew it my life was a mess. I realized I had to eat healthy not only for the sake of losing weight but also to have enough for my mind. Obviously, the challenge was not to stop eating more but to eat the right food, which I didn't like at all — but looking at the benefits that were at stake I had to try bit by bit to change.

The journey wasn't easy but a real struggle. I had to struggle each day. This is because one part of myself felt that I needed to change for my good while the other showed me that I was sacrificing my liking for the sake of the future. It is true that I needed to be healthy once again, but it was hard to overcome the strong urge of what I loved. It is much easier to replace what you don't like with what you do, but doing the opposite requires dedication and self-discipline.

This meant that I had to change how I perceived food. I knew that I needed my small weight back and so I had to do anything to achieve it. I had to work on my perception. I decided to value my body and decided if losing weight means eating what I didn't like, let it be so. I started taking the food I didn't like no matter the urge I had for sugary foods and chips. At first, it was not easy, but I constantly reminded myself of the benefits ahead. This made me step out further against my will. Having realized that our minds are not always set for success, but it is a practice that if embraced can bring results, I worked towards it.

After practicing the habit of eating what I don't like for a long time, I found that I no longer had many struggles in doing it. It now became much easier to eat the right food and my urge for sugary and junk foods reduced. This meant that I was now more in control of my life than before. I realized if I had done the easier thing of eating only what I liked no matter how harmful it was for my body; I could still be struggling with overweight.

After winning my bad eating habits, I realized that I was more disciplined in many areas of my life. I could no longer struggle to wake up and go to the gym for exercises. I was more focused on my goals, and therefore I achieved more. I have learned to exercise willpower and have a successful life. I came to realize that willpower is learned by practicing more often. You should not beat yourself when you realize that you lack the willpower to do something. Many people go through the same. What you should do is resist that temptation as much as you can. It may take a long time to overcome it, but if you persist, you will win. You will discover after you overcome your urge to eat unhealthy food, your willpower will start being stronger.

How Do You Discipline Your Eating Habit?

Set Realistic Goals

One mistake that people make when setting their goals is setting targets that are unattainable. You cannot wake up one morning and say that you will give up on the food that you have been eating for a long time instantly. It will only lead to frustration, and there is a high probability that you will give up. Let us have an example of exercising. It will be unrealistic to imagine that you can do exercises seven days a week when you are just starting out. However, you can manage to exercise four or five days a week. Instead of starting to eat all the things that you don't like, you can start by introducing one food at a time. Have short term targets that will make it easy to attain your long –term targets.

For instance, when losing weight, have in place Small targets that you would like to hit before going for your larger goal. You can purpose to lose two pounds per week and then increase a pound in the subsequent weeks. This will keep you motivated to step up towards attaining your main goal.

Keep Away the Food You Want to Avoid

It is easier than the next thing you will grab and eat is just in front of you. Imagine your kitchen is filled with foods that you want to avoid such as snacks and sugary foods. It will be easy for you to be tempted to eat them. Therefore, keeping them from your reach will help greatly in ensuring that you don't eat them. Fill your kitchen with foods that are healthy. Even if you don't like eating them, you will have no choice but to eat them.

Ensure Your Kitchen is Clean

I know this may sound crazy, but it is true. Eating entails a lot of self-discipline and self-control. The environment that you are in will determine how your minds perform. When you keep your kitchen messy, you are likely to eat more than if when in a clean environment. When in a clean environment your minds will be focused and organized, and you will be mindful of what you are eating.

Therefore, it is important no matter the kind of environment you are, ensure it is clean because it will help your mind to stay organized so that you can stay away from unnecessary cravings.

Unfollow Pages That Promote the Foods That You Are Avoiding

Today the internet can determine what you eat. Imagine you are following pages on the internet that are advocating the same foods you are trying to avoid. It will only worsen your struggle towards eating what you don't like. It is like watching porn videos and at the same time say that you are abstaining. It will be shockingly impossible. Therefore, if you want to eat healthily, start away from reading things that promote those foods that you are trying to avoid.

Your brain is affected by what you see and therefore if you want to win the war of unhealthy eating, follow pages and accounts that promote the kind of foods that you are trying to eat. Remember you are eating what you don't like and so keeping away from other foods that you like will greatly help.

Look for Your Motivation

This is so important when working towards your diet. Why are you eating food that you don't like? By answering this question, you will be motivated to continue pushing through. You are not doing this for the sake of punishing yourself. You may be working towards losing weight, staying healthy and more importantly build your self-discipline. Review your reasons for doing it and stick to it. Be specific in what you want and write it down. The main reason why people give up is because they forget their goal of doing something. Reminding yourself this reason will help you to refuse temptations to give up.

Avoid Stress

Stress is one of the reasons that cause you to eat foods that are not healthy. This is because when under stress you are not able to control yourself properly. You cannot imagine yourself eating what you don't like when you are a victim of stress. Stress takes control of a person that you no longer pay close attention to what is good or bad. This could be among the reasons why some people indulge in smoking and alcohol drinking when under stress. Despite knowing the harm smoking can cause, they still do it.

Therefore, being stress-free is significant in choosing what to eat and not to eat. Avoiding stress will enable you have more control of your life. You can reduce stress by practicing mindfulness, having enough sleep and eating healthy. After this, you will be able to eat food that you don't like for the sake of gaining self-discipline.

Exercise Mindfulness While Choosing Food and When Consuming

This means that before you consume any food, spend some time and think fully about it. Ask yourself, is this what my body requires, or it is just one of your cravings? This will allow you to choose what you eat well after you have considered all the benefits and consequences. If you find that despite liking a certain food, it will have long-lasting effects on your health, it will better to stop eating it. On the contrary, if there is a food that you hate, but it will work on your benefit, you will have no choice but to take it.

When you have decided on what to eat, don't be in a hurry while eating. You should experience pleasure while eating your food and so take the food slowly. When you exercise mindfulness while eating, it will not be easy to be addicted to food, and you will be proud concerning the food you have decided to eat, making you want to take it once more. Through this, you will find it easy to take that food more and more even though you didn't like it in the beginning.

The key to having self-discipline is doing the things we don't like so that you can achieve your goals. It may be that you don't like waking up early and do exercises or even practice mindfulness before going to your formal duties. But, looking at the benefits that will come from having such a habit, it will be right to give up on your sleep and do the right thing. Just like eating what you don't like for the sake of your health, you should go out of your comfort zone so that you can achieve your goals.

Your mind and your body will not always agree with what you must do, but you must ensure they do through exercise. When you have a clear picture of your expectations, don't let anything stand in your way. Don't be an enemy of yourself. Don't put hurdles for yourself when it is time to act. Sometimes your mind might tell that you are sacrificing your joy today because of what is unknown tomorrow, but you should not give in. Focus on your dreams more than you focus on your short-term pleasure, and you will see results.

Do not procrastinate on your dreams. Procrastination will deny you your opportunity to achieve greatness. Eliminate all distractions in your life and make sure each day you are making a step towards your achieving your goals.

The Procrastination Cure (It's Not Eat That Frog!)

Blueprint to Master Time with Highly Effective Strategies to Solving the Productivity Puzzle and Rid Yourself of Laziness with Atomic Habits

Chapter 1: The Reason You Procrastinate

One-fifth of the population procrastinates, and when you have such a negative impact on your life it diminishes your performance, affects your mental and physical health and increases your stress levels. This also makes you feel guilty and prolongs the timeframe you require to get tasks completed on a regular basis. It also affects the overall quality of the tasks. If you want to perform better and you do not want procrastination to affect the kind of work you do, it's important for you to find an effective solution.

There are several reasons why a person procrastinates, and it changes from person to person, which is why you need to first identify why you procrastinate in the first place. Once you identify the reason you procrastinate you will be able to work on it effectively and find the solution to a positive and healthy life.

You Lack Self-Compassion

If you do not have self-compassion, the tendency to stress always increases and this automatically increases the likelihood of procrastination.

People often wonder how they can suddenly introduce self-compassion to others. You can't! If you want to learn self-compassion you need to begin with yourself. Start talking kindly and motivate yourself even if you do something wrong. Instead of being a negative critic, start being positive and induce optimistic thoughts.

If you want to introduce self-compassion you must make sure that you practice forgiveness and stay open to the idea of forgiving yourself for the mistakes you make. Everyone makes mistakes in their life and at the end of the day you need to remind yourself that the mistakes you make are stepping stones towards learning on how to improve situations. Feeling bad about mistakes is not going to work well because this doesn't do you any good and it will only increase the chance of procrastination.

Always express gratitude because this is something that will ensure you introduce positive feelings inside of you and overcome your shortcomings as well. Gratitude is a great way to introduce self-compassion and is one of the most effective ways to teach yourself kindness as well. Generosity is another thing that will help increase self-compassion. The minute you become generous you start feeling positive and clear the clutter which gives you more space to think and take out the negativity from your life.

You Learned It from Someone

Procrastination is seldom self-taught which means you've either seen others behave in a particular manner and it has affected your ability to rationalize, or you've seen others demonstrate procrastination in front of you and learned to do the same, which is not healthy.

Sometimes you unknowingly latch on to information and behave in a particular manner. It's about learning how to unlearn what you realize is wrong. Positive people can bring about positive impacts in your life while negative people will make you feel low and sad. If you keep on thinking negative thoughts, then you won't manage to move on and teach yourself to become successful. You need to identify the root cause of your sorrows and why you keep feeling low so that you can work towards changing that and becoming a positive person. Procrastination has a lot to do with your emotions, and when you are emotionally drained or upset about something it becomes very difficult for you to feel good. This takes up most of your time and instead of planning how you will get things done you, you simply let the negativity take over your mind from time to time. This is not how you should function because it will eventually lead to self-destruction. Teach yourself to behave positively and find a role model who can teach you the right things.

You Underestimate Yourself

One of the major signs of procrastination is that you always underestimate yourself. While there is no clear explanation as to why people who procrastinate do this, they always do. Even if you're great at something, you will question your ability to be able to complete the task and start looking for the smallest errors once the task is complete. Some people don't even attempt doing something they could get done well because of procrastination.

Instead of trying to underestimate yourself you need to start motivating yourself and encourage yourself to do something you know you can attempt. Even if it turns out bad the first time, think about it as a learning experience and move on. Instead of feeling sorry for yourself you must learn and get better with each step you take. One of the root causes of procrastination is that you constantly believe you can't handle anything that you are asked to and no matter how hard you try you will deliver poor results, which is why people don't even try to attempt tasks that they could have done. Instead of underestimating yourself you need to teach yourself to get better.

You Can't Challenge Yourself

Unfortunately, one of the reasons you can't move ahead is because you continue to procrastinate. It's a never-ending cycle and until you learn how to break out of it, you may find yourself going around in circles.

If you want to overcome procrastination, it is important for you to continue challenging yourself and keep an open mind towards new things and accepting change. People who procrastinate are generally afraid of change and don't like to try new things since they believe they are not going to be good at it. Challenges are important for you to grow, and if you don't challenge yourself on a regular basis you will never manage to do well for yourself. One of the best ways to encourage yourself to try something new each day is to ensure you not only understand the importance of challenges but also how well they can work for you. While you may not want to challenge yourself at the start, once you do you will enjoy doing so, and this helps you get better at the things you do. Regularly challenging yourself also helps you to identify new ways to teach yourself something you never knew how to do. This is simple and effective, and it helps you get over procrastination. Challenges help you grow, and they are something you need to incorporate regularly to train your brain to get better and move higher up on the ladder of success.

Accurate Time Estimations

Most people procrastinate because they are not sure how long it will take to do certain tasks. Some people usually underestimate how quickly they can get things done and they often end up leaving work until the last minute. The main cause for this reason is overconfidence in your ability. Most people feel they will be able to manage tasks within a certain time frame even if they skip a couple of days in preparing for the task. This can come back to haunt you if the task turns out to be more difficult than you imagined or if it is something requires a lot of time to complete.

The best way to avoid this is to start earlier than planned and try to complete the task before the deadline. This will take care of any inaccurate time estimations and you can reward yourself with the time left on hand once you finish a task before schedule.

One of the major reasons for procrastination is that people end up with wrong time estimations, believing that they will be able to complete a job in no time at all. A realistic time frame is very important and without his time frame, not only will you end up delaying your tasks at hand, but you will also miss out on deadlines which will not leave a good impact on the person who is expecting the task complete from you. Proper time management is essential for you to move ahead and work towards success by overcoming procrastination. Don't underestimate how fast time flies because you need to manage it in the most effective way possible if you want a good and positive outcome.

Focusing on The Present Rather Than the Future

Most procrastination behaviors stem from the fact that people want their presence to be fruitful. People do not think too much about the future if they are able to procrastinate today. This usually results in quitting certain tasks if things become too difficult to handle.

You can avoid this by thinking about how your future can benefit from you working hard today. Getting an extra day to rest today is not really going to help you work harder and secure your future. You can't live for today, because at the end of the day if you don't plan your future you are not going to make your way to success. One of the most important things you need to remember when it comes to procrastinating is that if you live in the present without thinking about the future you won't be able to plan successfully, and you will constantly wonder if you have achieved anything. Planning is essential and without proper planning, you will not be able to achieve what you set out to do. Learn to plan your day effectively so you can use time more effectively, not just for the present but also for the future. After all, what you plan to create today can help you secure a better and more fruitful future.

Perfectionism

Another reason for procrastination is the importance of getting things done perfectly. This need for perfection often keeps you from starting work and this leads to delays and eventual failures to complete the work in hand.

Make sure you look back on your past examples where you have strived for perfection and not completed a task on time. This will give you enough motivation to complete tasks efficiently rather than perfectly. Stop trying to be perfect as it is impossible for you to perfect every task that you face. When you start targeting perfectionism it becomes difficult for you to stay focused on a task and get it completed effectively. No one will look solely for perfection in a task. What they look for is an effective result that can benefit them in the long run. Come up with solutions that will benefit you to save time and deliver more results rather than trying to perfect it. You won't be able to grow when you spend too much time on one particular task, but when you start handling multiple tasks you not only manage to expand your horizons but also grow as a person and become more successful. Focus on time management and efficiency rather than perfectionism.

Mental Illness Causing A Delay

Mental illnesses such as anxiety and depression can cause a delay in work. When you are suffering from depression or anxiety, you will not be able to focus on your work and your motivation will also likely be low.

Ensure treatment methods and therapy is incorporated into your life if you are not able to focus on work. If there are certain physical aspects that are causing your mood swings, you need to make sure you take care of those aspects before you start focusing on work again.

Procrastination is not easy to overcome but it is impossible to get over the tendencies of procrastination either. All you need to do is choose an effective path and have patience for it to work in your favor. There is no denying that procrastination limits your efforts to become productive, but it tricks you into feeling that this is not going to work, and you would only end up promising yourself things you never do. A smarter solution is to attempt small changes first and then go ahead with bigger changes once you have gotten used to the small changes you made. Through the process, you must keep motivating yourself and telling yourself that you can become better, more successful, and efficient in what you do by making simple changes in your life. Determination is important because motivation may not last forever, but determination will if you keep reminding yourself how important it is for you to stop procrastinating.

Dreadful Effects of Procrastination

People often underestimate how much procrastination can affect your life. If you were thinking that this is something you can deal with without having to struggle and without it affecting your regular day to day life, then you are sadly mistaken. Procrastination has a lot of negative effects on your life and when you learn to overcome them you will manage to see how much potential you have and what you can do with your goals by overcoming procrastination and focusing on success.

You Will Lose Precious Time

When you procrastinate on something you tend to put away any tasks that you have in hand irrespective of how close the deadline is. Instead of using time as your strength it becomes your biggest weakness because you wait until the last minute to get everything done and constantly regret it. Procrastination makes you feel low, and when you are in a negative state of mind it becomes difficult for you to turn that into something positive. A lot of people don't realize how much procrastination can affect you and they often think that they are simply getting distracted by certain scenarios in life and they need to deal with them before they can focus on work. The truth is that if you are procrastinating, something that is disturbing you today is more than likely to disturb you tomorrow, and even if that problem is sorted out it will keep coming up and you will still constantly be affected by it thereby making it difficult for you to work.

You Blow Off Opportunities

People look forward to an opportunity that can help them change their life, but unfortunately, they procrastinate and don't even realize these opportunities when they come knocking at their door because they are so busy complaining about the problems that they are going through. Most of the time, people don't even realize how they have given up on an opportunity because of ignorance and constant complaining. If you are always in a negative state of mind it will be very difficult for you to see something positive and you tend to ignore an opportunity that might be great for your career.

You Will Not Meet Your Goals

No matter how easy the task at hand is, people who procrastinate find it exceedingly difficult to keep up with their daily schedule and they always end up missing a deadline or delaying it. This is not because you have less time on hand. It is because you spent most of your time complaining. The worst thing about people that procrastinate is that it becomes difficult for them to identify the procrastination that's occurring regularly, and they only realize it when it's too late. Unless you have self-discipline implemented in your life you will not be able to realize how difficult it is for you to keep up with your daily tasks

It Could Ruin Your Career

People who procrastinate tend to snap because they are always in a negative mood and this doesn't benefit them because most of the time it works out against them. When you are constantly upset about things around you, you can't see the good in anyone or anything and this could put your job at risk because it makes it difficult for you to get along with the people you work with. Since you already delay your work and you are not able to keep up with the task at hand, there is a higher chance that you may end up losing the job because of your behavior. Procrastination generally ruins much more than you could even imagine and the sooner you identify the problem the more in control you will be and manage to take care of the situation.

It Lowers Your Self-Esteem

It lowers your self-esteem and makes you feel bad about yourself. Even if you are highly talented and skilled you will never be able to put your skill and talent to good use because you always feel that you are not worth it, and you will not be able to do anything effectively. The feeling of negativity usually grips you and you automatically believe that you aren't good at anything and no matter how hard you try you will not manage to achieve success. Ironically, people who procrastinate generally don't put in too much effort and although they believe they do, they do very little towards the job which is why they don't get it done as effectively.

Poor Decisions

When you are not in a proper frame of mind you will never manage to figure out what decisions are in favor of you and what are the kind of decisions you shouldn't take. Sometimes your decisions are even made just so that you can add stress upon yourself and see just to see how much emotional pressure you can handle. While a person who does not procrastinate will look towards taking a decision that will make them happy, people who procrastinate generally look to bring more sorrow into their life by making a tough choice.

Damage Your Reputation

People who procrastinate get labeled as being lazy and unable to get a job done on time. They also get labeled as being arrogant and annoying and people who do not get along with others that easily. While you may believe that this is your nature or the character that you have it's not so. it's because you are procrastinating, and you haven't realized it yet. Procrastination has a lot of negative effects on your life and the sooner you identify these problems the easier it will be for you to deal with them. There is a cure for everything and once you know that you are procrastinating you can work towards treating it effectively.

You Risk Your Health

People who procrastinate tend to spend most of their time doing almost nothing and then become lethargic and lazy. It also increases their stress and anxiety levels, and this causes various problems including increased risk of depression. People who procrastinate may get depressed because of their inability to complete tasks and this usually is a reason why they may spend time alone. Being alone can put them at high risk to succumb to various other mental illnesses. Depression can potentially ruin your life and unless you do something to work towards treating it you will not be able to lead a productive life.

If you do not want procrastination to take over your life, it's important for you to identify you are procrastinating and take the necessary measures to work towards fighting it.

Chapter 2:
Productivity Secrets to Dominate

Procrastination is not easy to overcome which is why a lot of people struggle with it for a long time. If you want to overcome procrastination you got to identify your skills and enhance them the right way so that you can convert your weaknesses into your strengths and start benefiting from it. People often wonder how they can overcome procrastination and what needs to be done in order to do so. I will let you in on some effective secrets that work well to overcome procrastination and lead you on the path of success.

Empty Your Mind

It is important for you to clear up physical clutter so that you will be able to work more effectively or do something productive - it's the same with your mind. If there are a lot of thoughts in your head, this won't help you in any way and it will make it tough to focus on one topic because there so many things going on in your head. For you to begin your journey against procrastination, you need to learn how to control what you think about and prioritize your thoughts. It may sound silly, but some people end up procrastinating over the smallest things and waste time complaining instead of doing something about it. You need to understand there are two situations in life - the ones you can control and the ones you can't. Here's what you need to remember - you are only in control of your thoughts and no matter how much you would like to change the way a person thinks about you or what they say about you, it's not in your hands. Instead of worrying about what people have to say, try diverting that energy into doing something beneficial for yourself. Stressing about situations you can't control makes no sense because it will make you feel bad and you will continue procrastinating. The best way to get back at people who talk about you or make you feel bad about yourself is to complete something and become successful. If you want to do that, you need to start by clearing your thoughts and prioritizing what's important and making your mind sharper.

Have a day just to yourself

This benefits you a great deal because it helps you think effectively without disturbing you in any way. You are what you need to do. Have one day during the week where you avoid doing any tasks at all. If you sit down to work and you notice that you often get distracted by your cellphone or social media networking sites, make it a point to not use those gadgets or websites for one day. This doesn't mean you start living off the grid and avoid your phone completely. While you can use your phone to make phone calls when necessary, stop scrolling through the messages or using it for other purposes other than calls.

If you are addicted to talking to people over the phone, have a time limit on the number of phone calls as well as the duration of the calls during that free day. What this does is it helps you to stay focused and stops you from getting sidetracked by unnecessary activities that eat into your time in which you could have invested in doing something beneficial and fruitful for yourself. It's not easy to give up something you are addicted to which is why you should set one day aside to fulfill your needs so that you motivate yourself towards working hard and getting one step closer to success. You must remember that success comes at a price and it isn't easy to get. The more effort you put, the higher the rewards you reap.

Prioritize Your Work

While the first step in prioritizing your work is to clear your mind and ensure that you only focus on what is important, you need to spend the time to sort out work based on what is more important or less important. There are very repetitive tasks that you will have to do daily, and these will be your regular tasks which you have to get done. If you want to make the most out of your time, then you should try to finish up your regular tasks faster so you have more time on hand as well as energy to focus on important tasks that can help you become successful. There are many things on which you will waste time on a regular basis, and you may want to figure out where you are investing that time so you will be able to cut down on the distractions and prioritize more effectively. Prioritizing your tasks also helps you identify where you are eating up into your time and how small changes in your routine you can give you more time to focus on becoming successful. When you prioritize your time and there's an important task, you can focus on it more effectively and this means that you are putting in quality as well as quantity towards the task, thereby increasing the chances of being highly successful.

Break Down Your Time

Instead of working consistently for a long period of time, you need to try to break down your tasks into multiple sections that are no longer than 15 to 20 minutes each. After each successful completion of a task you can move on to the next. With this method you can then focus on small portions of the bigger task and ensure that you get them done well. 15 minutes seems like a short amount of time to get work done, but you start focusing more effectively. This helps to increase your productivity without putting too much stress on you. It is also important for you to take a break in between your work session which means if you have 3 back-to-back tasks you should give yourself one break before you resume the fourth task. This not only helps you in terms of energy, it helps you to calm your mind and focus as you did on the first task. Time management is very important when it comes to beating procrastination but it's important for you to realize it takes time. Make it a habit to break down certain tasks into multiple portions so you can make better use of time.

Choose Your Thinking Position or Place

There are a lot of people who manage to think better when they are in a place or position. Instead of limiting yourself to your office desk you should see where you are most comfortable and where you feel most relaxed. That is probably the place you will be most creative and be able to think and brainstorm for the best ideas that can benefit you and help you become successful.

Maintain an Unlimited to Do List

Almost everyone has a to-do list, and sometimes this list gets so lengthy it is impossible for you to keep up with the never-ending task list. While it's good to have a to-do list, it's important for you to prioritize that list and mark tasks based on whether they are less important or more important. Always begin with the ones that are most important or have restricted time frames so you can focus on the other less important tasks with the remaining time you have left. You should prepare a to-do list in such a way that the tasks that are important should be completed during the day you receive it and the least important ones can be left for other days. It's all about finding your rhythm - where you decide what must be done at the start of the day when you have the most energy and where you are more focused, and what can be left for the end of the day that doesn't require too much of your attention. Practical thinking always works because if you want to become successful you need to make practical decisions by keeping in mind tasks that will benefit you.

Don't Pressure Yourself

Let's face it; we all have so much to do yet so little time that it can be daunting. It's important for you to draw a line every day and decide that this is how much work you can handle and nothing more. When you take up too much work or more work than you can handle it affects your productivity and quality of work, which means it will take you nowhere. There is a difference between working smarter and working harder which is why you need to limit the amount of work you do based on your ability to cope and the time you have. Sometimes a task could be completed in less than 2 hours, but it could drain you out of your energy completely which means you need to rest before you start a new task, especially if you want to get it done just as well as you did the previous task. Just because something can be completed in 2 hours doesn't mean you take up multiple such jobs for an 8-hour work schedule. Remember, you need to account for break time too. Most of these tasks will be done during your peak hours and it will be the cause of low energy levels and lack of focus. Breaks are important and you have to consider the amount of time your body takes to relax and rejuvenate before you get back to work so you can maintain quality.

Make A Daily Action Plan

Your to-do list doesn't have to be everything that you do daily; there can always be something spontaneous on your agenda. This could be anything from treating yourself after a well-worked week or challenging yourself to do a little more on a Monday just see you how much you can push yourself. You need to remember that your daily actions that may or may not be successful, but that doesn't have to disrupt your routine. You simply need to change the way you think and approach the situation. It's something that can help you better yourself or figure out what needs to be changed and whether there is room for improvement.

Prioritize the Difficult Projects First

When you start your day, you need to make sure that you prioritize your work and note it down based on urgency and difficulty. If there are many tasks to complete that don't require a lot of time to complete, then you should start with the most difficult tasks first. Once the worst is out of the way it will give you enough time to complete the rest of the tasks that are relatively easier, and you will have less stress as well. Prioritizing not only helps you complete all the tasks at hand, but it will also ensure that you think with a clear mind and do not handle too many tasks at the same time. Starting with these later and keeping the difficult ones for the end of the day will make your day extremely difficult. You will continue dreading the moment when the difficult tasks need to be completed and this will keep you demotivated throughout the day.

Two-Minute Rule

The two-minute rule was introduced by none other than David Allen. This rule is extremely simple. When you are handed a task, take a moment to figure out whether it can be completed within 2 minutes or not. If it can be completed in two minutes, then you should do it immediately. This will reduce the length of your task list and it will take a lot off your plate once you start implementing this properly. The only flipside to this rule is you should not start doing tasks in two minutes just for the heck of it. If a task requires time, make sure you give it ample time and do justice to the work that has been assigned to you. The way this works is that it helps you to work in small intervals and this keeps you motivated throughout. You tend to get more done when you look at work in two-minute intervals and it helps you be more productive. When there are a ton of small and minor jobs that need to get done, you will manage to complete them without any delays or procrastination because in a mere two minutes there's not a lot of time left for you to think. It's like a constant challenge where you push yourself to finish multiple tasks during the day. While these small tasks don't seem like much, when they accumulate it tends get to you and you feel pressurized to finish them. The two-minute rule helps you knock the small tasks out of the way systematically and leaves only the big tasks pending.

Assign A Work Area

If you work in an office, it goes without saying that you would have a cubical that would be assigned to you and you would be expected to work from this space. If you work from home, then you need to make sure that you segregate your work life from your personal life. It can be very easy to sit on the couch and write if you work from home, but this will compromise the integrity of the task at hand and you will not be able to complete it accurately. Even when you work from home you need to make sure that you assign a workspace and that space should be used only for your work and nothing else. Your comfort level is important while you work but it does not mean that you get so comfortable that you end up procrastinating and taking a quick power nap.

One of the worst things you can do when you work from home is to plonk yourself on the bed to work. Sitting on your bed with your laptop is the least productive way to get things done since you'll never feel like you're working. When you work you've got to put your energy into focusing on the task and this can't be done in a casual place, like your bed, where you rest and relax most of the time. It's all about creating the right mindset in order to get more work done.

If you work from home, you should always take the time to build your own workspace. This needs to be a separate space and should in no way be connected to your comfort zone or the space you spend time relaxing. You also need to make sure this space is not too close to the television or other recreational activities such as your gaming console or even your mp3 player. Having these distractions close to your workspace is a strong temptation and when you look at these gadgets, you'll feel like utilizing them. When you work, you need to stay focused on what you do and the only way you'll be able to do this is when you stay away from these distractions. When it's out of sight, it's usually out of your mind too. So, try to keep these distractions out of your sight when you're working.

Peak Working Hours

When you work a 9 to 5 schedule, there would be certain hours of the day that you would be most productive and other times that you would not deliver as much work as expected. The same would be the case when you are working from home. If you feel that 9 to 5 is not your cup of tea, then you could decide your golden hours for work and work according to that schedule. There are people that work from home and sleep through the day while working at night. This helps keep away all the distractions and they can work peacefully. Some people even start their work in the afternoon and end up working until late in the evening. No matter what schedule you stick to, you need to make sure that you are alert during that time, and you cross maximum things off your list. Once you have decided your peak working hours you need to make sure that you stick to that and not change your schedule too often.

Figuring out what time you're most productive is key. If you haven't figured it out yet, take time to try working at odd hours for a few days and see the time you found most comfortable to work. There are several people who aren't aware about the hours they are most productive at and often stumble upon it by accident. If you want to learn about your golden hours, you need to stretch your work hours for a few days to figure it out.

Eliminate Distractions

If you need to complete certain tasks within a limited time frame then you may want to eliminate all distractions in your work environment. One of the biggest distractions these days is the internet. If you just need to sit down and write, then you may want to pretend that you are in an airplane and the internet connectivity is very limited. You should also pretend that your cell phone does not function. This will allow you to work without any kind of interruption and it will keep you very focused.

Putting your phone away can help increase productivity by a great extent. Not only does it allow you to focus better, you end up saving a ton of time and manage to get the job done faster when your phone is away.

Be Consistent

The key to success is always staying on top of your game and continuing to work as soon as you finish the previous task. The most successful writers in the world started writing their new book as soon as they finished their previous one. They don't wait to read feedback they receive for the book because they believe in their work, so they continue writing. Successful writers make it a point to write a minimum of 2000 words daily. This keeps the creativity flowing and it also ensures that the work never stops. When you work continuously, the momentum will be in your favor.

When you're not consistent with what you do, you end up with different results for each day. This means you won't be able to judge whether you're delivering the kind of work you want. You don't have to push yourself to your limits every day. When you have a schedule planned and when you stick to it, you will end up being more productive without struggling to meet deadlines and without having to stay up for long hours.

Take Care of Your Health

While you may feel that you need to work all the time and not take any breaks, you should make sure that you do not experience burn out. The endeavor to be successful should not be so fierce that you end up falling ill. Take enough breaks through the day and take at least one day off during the week. This will not only help protect your body, but it will also protect your frame of mind.

If you want to perform well, you've got to stay healthy and look after yourself. If you're not healthy, you'll end up missing out on a few days of work and this will hinder your progress along with your commitment to staying consistent. Try to give yourself a break every now and then. Always remember, the minute you feel the pressure is getting to you, relax. The key to performing well long term is to understand when you need to stop for a while before you resume the task at hand.

Try Various Methods

If you have been working hard and you are not getting the right kind of results, then you need to try and change your working style. What may have worked for someone else will not necessarily work for you. Always look to innovate with your work and do something different daily. When your working style becomes monotonous, it will reflect in the results. Changing your working methods regularly will ensure you always stay excited about your work and have different methods to work with each time.

Living by the book may not be the best solution for everyone. While a few things work well for some, it might not be the best solution for another. It may take you awhile to find something that works, so keep experimenting with different methods until you find your mojo and once you do, stick to it.

Procrastination is more common than you can imagine and due to this, there are several misconceptions that are related to how you should be able to overcome procrastination effectively. If you want to increase self-discipline and you want to walk the path of success, you need to make sure you differentiate between what is myth and what will work. Here are a few myths that you should not believe regarding procrastination.

#1 - I Work Better Under Pressure

Pressure seldom brings out the best in you and while you may create an illusion that you are working really hard and efficiently because you are pressured for time, the truth is that you will end up making a lot of mistakes because you want to get the job done faster rather than more efficiently. While there are a few people who tend to work well under pressure, this isn't something one should do regularly since it takes a toll on your health. While working under pressure may help you get the kind of results you're aiming for, you won't be able to pull this off for long. Working under pressure will drain you out and you will eventually get tired. This will start affecting your overall productivity and you won't be able to keep up to the growing demands of your work.

When under pressure, you try working faster on a task and there's a possibility you will try to cut the job short and take shortcuts. This may not work out to benefit the project. It all begins when you start procrastinating and delaying work, leaving it all until the last minute. Procrastination will harm your overall performance and it won't help you to perform better because pressure leads to stress and stress leads to silly mistakes that will be reflected in your work.

Don't convince yourself that you do well under pressure, instead convince yourself to work well in a systematic way where there is no pressure and where you enjoy doing what you do. It is important for you to remember that enjoying what you do matters more than anything because that's when you start doing work that is good quality and will get you credit for. Pressure doesn't do that.

#2 - I Need Inspiration to Work

You may not have inspiration every day of your life, but you still must work every day if you want to get closer to your goal. You can't just wait to 'get in the mood' but rather you must create the mood and motivate yourself to work well every day.

You also need to tell yourself not all days are the same and you may feel great on certain days but that there are days that may not be that well-organized and there will be times you may get frustrated or upset. However, that's not the reason for you to stop working, but rather for you to push yourself and remind yourself that you should work because you have a stipulated time frame and an agenda you have to stick to, rather than letting the day go to waste just because of negative emotions.

You can't expect others to inspire you all the time and while you can try to change circumstances a little and create a more positive work environment it begins from within you. You must be the source of your inspiration rather than depending on anybody else to be that for you. Inspiring yourself is easier than having to depend on another person to do so and it also gets you more in control of your emotions which means you will be able to take control of the tasks in hand and not let your feelings affect the outcome.

#3 - Needing Three or Four Hours of Uninterrupted Time

This is a very common myth that several people use as an excuse in order to delay work that is being done by them. There are several ways that you can stop procrastination and do a lot of work in very little time. You need to save little chunks of time from various other tasks and then use the chunks together to complete a difficult or a massive task. It is very difficult to find large chunks of time available if you lead a very busy life. Waiting for a large portion of uninterrupted time is just an excuse to procrastinate your work because you know that chunk is not going to be available. If you keep waiting until the last minute you will then pressure yourself to complete the task quickly and before you know it, you will end up performing poorly.

There are several rules that you can follow in order to get difficult tasks completed well within the time frame. You need to use these rules to your advantage. One of the things you can do is use the Swiss cheese approach in order to break down large tasks. If you have seen a Swiss piece of cheese you will know that there are several holes in it - this is what you need to get done with your tasks. Poke small holes into your tasks and reduce the demands of the task over a period. The small holes could be in the form of time that you take out from your busy schedule to complete a portion of that big task. The biggest fear that people have is starting a task and not realizing the sheer volume of the task. Once you have begun working on a task, you will realize that the task was not as difficult as you expected it to be. When you start poking holes into a task you will make constant progress and you will end up finishing the task with ease.

You need to make use every minute that you have when you have a busy schedule. If you have 30 minutes to spare after your lunch hour, you can ask yourself what can be done within that time frame. Do not look at your task as a large chunk of work that needs to be completed. When you break down your tasks in two portions, you will be able to finish it one bit at a time with the small chunks of time that you have been able to spare throughout your day.

#4 - I Will Do A Better Job Later

Yes, we all have made this mistake of thinking that tomorrow is going to be a better day. How often do we procrastinate because we were just too scared to take up tasks today? It is very easy to sit down and think that tomorrow you will be able to do a better job because you will be better organized, and you will have more control over the tasks. However, the truth remains that unless you start doing a task today you will not be productive tomorrow. If you were running short on time today, you will run out of time tomorrow as well. If you are not disciplined today, you will never be disciplined anytime soon. Start pushing yourself and get work done today. Yes, it will take a little bit of effort and it will need a little bit of coaxing from within, but you need to get it done. Avoid using this excuse because this is one of the worst procrastination myths and you will never get out of this vicious cycle. Your proposed tomorrow will never come, and you will never be able to complete any of the tasks that you have to do.

Most of us use some or all these myths on a daily basis and we continue delaying the tasks that we have. Just because a task makes you feel uncomfortable, it doesn't mean you need to be afraid of it. Sometimes even a complex task can turn out to be one of the easiest ones on your list. Don't be overwhelmed by the things that you do because if you do not do the task, someone else will. If you want to move ahead in life and be successful, you cannot let others take over your responsibilities as this will not put you in a good light. Stop putting yourself down and be confident in your ability to work on important and difficult tasks. It's time to kick these myths out the window.

Chapter 3: The 10 Minute Rule Guaranteed to Work

Several people tend to put off tasks that cause them physical discomfort or emotional discomfort and that's when they begin procrastination. It could be as small as not wanting to talk to somebody over the phone or planning a daily schedule that you are forced to follow. Although most people believe that getting over procrastination is a tough task, the truth is you need to make the right decisions and stay determined to do so. The 10-minute rule is something that a lot of people believe works very well to overcome procrastination, and this is something I back completely. It's easy to follow, simple, and highly effective.

How to Use The 10-Minute Rule?

The 10-minute rule is simple, all you need to do is tell yourself that you are going to focus on working on a task uninterrupted for 10 minutes. Once you reach the 10-minute mark you will ask yourself again whether you want to keep going for another 10 minutes and continue if you decide you want to. At the end of the 10 minutes when you question yourself about continuing the task or not, you will end up continuing for at least 9 of those times you challenge yourself. This means that without forcing yourself to get something done, you will manage to increase productivity in an effective way.

The 10-minute rule is a great way to overcome procrastination and push yourself to work a little more each time. When you convince yourself to work for 10-

minutes, you end up feeling good in the process and you automatically want to do more once you start. This not only helps you to work more consistently, but also more efficiently.

Why This Rule Works

Most people stress about getting a short task done and dread the moment they need to start the task. The 10-minute rule allows you to work for 10 minutes at a time, which will make the total time seem like a small amount of time to invest in. You can decide whether you want to continue with another 10-minute task at the end of the 10th minute and so on. This illusion of working for just 10 minutes motivates you to work and you start immersing yourself in the task without realizing how many hours go by.

The 10-minute rule helps you to focus on tasks that you aren't even interested in doing and ensure that you get it done in an effective way. It helps you to overcome the negative feelings and the feelings of anxiety that you normally go through when you are not confident about starting a task.

Convince yourself that you need to invest only 10 minutes in doing something you started with a positive mindset, and once you start performing the task you are motivated to finish it. Doing this on a regular basis will not only help increase productivity, but it also improves the quality of work that you deliver thereby getting you a little closer to success. When you incorporate the 10-minute rule into your daily life you start eliminating procrastination completely.

It's All About Getting Started

Before you begin, all you need to do is ask yourself whether you are ready to challenge yourself for the next 10 minutes, and before you know it, you will manage to do it effectively. Here are three steps that will come handy in implementing the 10-minute rule:

Delegate Work

Delegation has been the most successful way of managing work and time. There are certain managers that are excellent at what they do, and they never seem to say no to any task assigned to them. Delegation has several benefits and you need to make sure that you use this method to the fullest. When you start assigning work to others, your to-do list will keep decreasing and you will have ample time to focus on the important tasks at hand. This is where the 10-minute rule can be implemented excellently. Take a moment to study your to-do list and make sure that you delegate all the tasks that can be completed within 10 minutes. This will help you complete all tasks within the deadline and ensure that you are doing so without any stress.

Delegated work may sound easy, but it is not. There are times when you end up not delegating a certain task because you are not sure how the other person will deliver. You need to remember one simple rule - completing a task well is better than completing it perfectly. There will always be imperfections, even in your own work. The only way you can succeed is by moving ahead and letting go of things. When you start delegating work you will be able to take on additional responsibilities and new projects. This will help you learn and grow in your career. If you continue doing the same tasks daily you will never progress, and you will remain at an entry-level position. If you are looking to get promoted, you need to find somebody that can do your current job. If you are irreplaceable at your current job, the management will never promote you because they feel that no one else can do the tasks that you are currently doing.

Delegating will show that you are capable of trusting others and you will be interested in taking up more responsibilities by higher management.

Break Up the Tasks

You should know that almost every task can be broken up into 10-minute microtasks. This will help you complete a two-hour task in just 30 minutes. For example, you need to come up with a new plan to improve sales in your organization. You can break this task up into several 10-minute microtasks. Take the first 10 minutes and figure out how you can get new ideas. Once you have jotted down new ideas, you can take another 10 minutes and log on to the internet to try and elaborate on these ideas. Once that is done, take another 10 minutes and get everyone gathered near your desk for a brainstorming session. While the brainstorming session may not be completed within 10 minutes, you have completed the planning phase of the task at hand in less than an hour and this is how a 10-minute rule can prove to be effective to you.

The 10-minute rule can also be implemented in your personal life. If you have been reaching the office late daily, you need to figure out your morning routine and see what can be changed. Break down all your morning tasks into 10 minutes and this will help you get organized a lot quicker. Try brushing your teeth and washing your face in 10 minutes, taking a shower in 10 minutes, eating your breakfast in 10 minutes and gathering all your things together to leave the house in 10 minutes. These are some of the major tasks that you carry out in the morning and all of it can be completed in less than an hour. This is the power of the 10-minute rule.

Use A Timer

Several people try to implement the 10-minute rule however they fail because they lose track of time and 10 minutes turn into 2 hours. When you are in a high-stress situation at work, time can fly, and you need to make sure that you stick to the 10-minute rule in order to make time your best friend. always Keep a timer with you - these days it is very easy because almost every smartphone has an inbuilt timer. Time each of your tasks that you are striving to complete under 10 minutes and see where you are falling behind.

The only way you can maximize productivity is by pushing yourself and trying to complete tasks within the allotted time frame. While certain tasks may go beyond 10 minutes, you should not let it linger on until you lose complete track of time and do not complete the task at all. Keeping track of time will help you improve over a period and you will become a lot more efficient. At the end of the day, you need to keep experimenting with the various time frames that work best for you and stick to the 10-minute rule. You may not be able to be as motivated as you want to the first time, but the secret is to just keep going until you find your rhythm and manage to use it to your advantage.

Chapter 4:
Fool Proof Method to Breaking Bad Habits

Procrastination can cause you to delay a lot of your tasks because of the feeling of laziness and putting off things on your to-do list until the end of the day. If you want to overcome procrastination, it's important that you do the right thing and learn how to break habits that hamper your efficiency. You also need to understand that it's not something which will happen within a few days but rather something that needs effort, invested time, as well as determination for you to figure out the most effective ways to be productive and overcome procrastination. There is a lot that you can do to achieve better results within the same time frame. It all involves using methods that work well for you and understanding the importance of making the most out of your time rather than spending it worrying about whether you will be able to get something done on time.

Breaking the Task into Smaller Steps

One of the major reasons people procrastinate is because they find it extremely difficult to get the job done since it seems too overwhelming to complete. While some tasks are small, others may require you to invest a lot of time and the fear of having to deal with such a big project may lead you to procrastinate. Instead of pondering over how you're going to accomplish a big task, it makes more sense for you to break it down into smaller portions so that you don't need to look at it is a big project.

Let's take the example of writing a book and break it down into phrases that will make it easy for you to complete the task at hand. You could include the following phases:

- Research
- Narrowing down the topic
- Creating an outline
- Drafting the content
- Writing the chapters
- Proofreading
- Adding the final touches

When you break down your work into smaller portions it seems to be more manageable and you are more able to get the job done on time. Once you have broken down your work into smaller portions you then need to dedicate time and ensure that you get everything done in your stipulated time frame, so you do not delay the project. Give yourself a realistic time frame so you don't end up getting things done last minute. It benefits you in the number of ways because it not only helps you to focus better but you end up delivering quality work that you will be proud of.

Change Your Environment

This may surprise you but different environments have different impacts regarding your productivity. If you suddenly feel demotivated in your workspace or when you are at home, try thinking about places that you believe will motivate you to do better. You can also experiment with new places where your productivity is at its peak. For some writers, coffee shops could be a great place to put on your thinking cap and come up with innovative ideas to write about. When you confine yourself to a space you don't allow yourself to unleash and think, and this leads to eventual procrastination. Sometimes when you spend too much time at home, the feeling of laziness starts to creep up and each time you look at your bed you may want to snuggle in and go for a quick nap. All of this can be avoided if you think smart and figure out places where you manage to work most effectively. If you like sitting in the library, try and spend as much time as you can there because it's one of the most effective places for you to focus on work. Libraries are quiet, there are no distractions, and you cannot talk which means you won't be distracted in any way and you will put in all your energy on work.

You can also head to a coffee shop to work. While you may think such a place would have a lot of distractions, it helps you relax and get creative. If you're used to a coffee shop, make it a point to visit the same one. There's something about familiar places that help you work better. If you haven't discovered your space yet, you need to explore the possible options that you think could work well for you. However, don't spend your day shifting from one coffee shop to another. If you think this will not work for you, try another alternative such as a library.

Create Your Own Deadlines

As mentioned in point one you should always dedicate a certain amount of time to each task and set a realistic deadline so you know you must have that task completed by that date. When you have too much work to handle but there are a lot of days before the deadline, you tend to take it easy for the first few days because you are not close to the deadline and psychologically you tend to believe you have enough time before you need to start your task. Unfortunately, people find it difficult to stick to deadlines because they avoid working for a few days and this creates a lot of stress. If you want to avoid all of this, you need to remember that apart from breaking down your tasks into smaller and easier jobs you also need to set deadlines for each task. If a task is relatively easy then give yourself a day or two to finish it, and if it's a little more difficult try assigning 3 to 4 days for you to finish the job. If the work requires about 15 to 20 days always give yourself at least two days off and during these two days make sure to pamper yourself so you are rejuvenated and motivated to get back to work.

Promise yourself that you will only take a day off when you complete a certain number of tasks on your list, so you know you are at par with your timeline. The final deadline that you pick should be at least a day prior to the actual deadline date because it's always important to give yourself a buffer and a little wiggle room.

In case something goes wrong or there's an emergency you need to tend to, you'll still manage to get the job done on time because of the buffer you gave yourself. If you finish the task before the actual deadline, you can always use the spare day to pamper yourself or relax. After all, you need to rest before you take on a new task if you want to continue performing well.

Eliminate Distractions

While some people tend to procrastinate when they are stressed, others procrastinate a little more frequently. If you realize you are procrastinating way too much and you are not able to focus on a task even after you are breaking it down and assigned it time, then you need to eliminate distractions and force yourself to focus. You need to eliminate all external distractions including your social media pages that you browse in between work hours and use a filter to block the sites or deactivate your accounts until you complete your tasks. While most people manage to take control over procrastination by setting certain deadlines and tasks that they should do on days, if you are unable to do that, then taking a drastic step may help you to focus and get back on track. Instead of deactivating your social media accounts, you can always ask a trustworthy friend to change your passwords and give them to you only after you have completed a certain number of tasks. This will help you motivate yourself to get the job done fast and without distractions and it becomes a lot easier for you to focus. Eliminating distractions is not difficult, what's difficult is to take the first step towards eliminating it because we are so dependent and addicted to these websites. Once you absorb yourself in work, you will not feel the need to go to the websites repeatedly and you manage to focus more on work and put your energy where it matters.

Hangout with People Who Inspire You

Try and stay away from bad influences. When you spend time with people who influence in a negative way you procrastinate. Similarly, when you spend time with people who have a positive impact on your life you start performing better because you are motivated to do well. When you look at highly successful people and what they have accomplished in their life you realize that it doesn't come easy. One of the most important things that they invested in was effort and long hours of unrestricted work. If you want to see yourself in their position or anywhere close to it, you must follow their footsteps and do things that makes you more productive rather than force you to procrastinate. A positive mindset has a positive impact on your life, and it will help you live a more fulfilling life that benefits you. You'll always have negative people in your life that will tell you to spend time doing things that won't benefit you in any way, but if you want to become successful, you must work hard and eliminate distractions including bad influences from your life.

It's shocking how much people can influence you and this doesn't just have to do with major distractions. It could even be something as small as forcing you to abandon your task to head out for a smoke break or just to engage in unnecessary gossip. While it's important for you to socialize, you need to know whom to socialize with and how much time you should invest in socializing. You should also consider spending time with people who inspire rather than annoy you. Make sure you spend time discussing ideas, not people.

Great Minds Discuss Ideas. Average Minds Discuss Events. Small Minds Discuss People. Personal Excellence.

Find A Friend or Companion

The one thing that will motivate you to work effectively and enjoy what you do is having a friend or a companion who shares the same interests and goals as you. When you have somebody to encourage you, not only do you manage to achieve your goals a lot faster, but you manage to execute a plan more effectively. It also helps you to assist each other during difficult times, and it manages to lift your spirit and brings you back on track. When you spend time with somebody who works with you, energy levels are always high, and this automatically brings out the best in the both of you. You can also learn how to delegate tasks together and come up with the most effective solutions to work towards achieving the goal as a team. When you have a partner, who has the same goals as you, you convert your work time to fun time and start enjoying what you do.

Tell Others About Your Goal

It's very important for you to let people know what you are doing and how proud you are of it. Whether it's your family members, your friends, colleagues, or even acquaintances, make sure you let them know about the project that you have taken up and just how motivated you are towards working and completing it on time. While you don't have to boast about how well you are doing, simply inform them about how motivated you are to get work done because not only will this convince you of your motivation levels but it will make you feel proud each time you talk about it and this will encourage you to work harder. Acknowledging what you do lessens procrastination and makes you more confident in doing the job. For you to be able to overcome feelings of anxiety or procrastination you have to be confident with your skills. One of the best ways to do it is to continuously talk about your plans and how you are going to execute them in a more effective way. When you talk about your goals don't worry about what other people say, just focus on letting them know what you plan to do. You also need to decide who you want to stop sharing information with. Sometimes people tend to put you down and if you get a feeling of negativity from somebody every time you try to tell him about your goal you may want to refrain from telling these people because they will only make you feel bad about yourself and you will begin procrastinating again.

Talk to Someone Who Has Achieved A Lot

As stated above, if you want to make the most out of your life you need to have a role model who inspires you and guides you in the right direction. This doesn't necessarily mean it has to be somebody who is a millionaire or is very rich but someone who is happy with life and content with what they have achieved. You must also remind yourself that success isn't only measured in terms of money but also in terms of how much somebody has done and how content they are with their life. You should look for someone you believe has achieved almost everything you would want and look up to them as a role model. Open and communicate with them so you can get ideas on how you should plan your goals and your life ahead. When you look up to somebody in a positive way and seek advice from them you can always ask for solutions that can help you become a better person.

Recheck Your Goals After A While

If you're haven't procrastinated for a while and you believe that you are getting better at being productive, then it's time for you to check on your goals and see how well you are doing. If it's getting too easy to complete tasks and you have a lot of spare time you may want to think about how you want to dedicate more time to performing better. At the end of the day, it is all about getting closer to your dream and becoming more focused towards success than ever before.

The more time you spend following the right ways to break from the habit of procrastination, the better you'll get, and this simply means that you should also challenge yourself a little more every time. After all, it's important for you to grow, and for you to do this, you must take a bigger step ahead every few months.

You should also set long term goals for yourself and recheck every few months to see whether you are achieving those goals or whether you have gotten any closer to them than you were a few months ago. When you get a certain amount of your goals achieved you should pamper yourself by giving yourself a day off, taking a holiday, or even buying something nice for yourself. It is important to reward yourself for the good work you do because that keeps you motivated to keep doing better so you can provide for yourself and for your family.

Don't Over Complicate Things

One of the worst habits of people who procrastinate is that they over-complicate things by continuously trying to make them better. You need to understand that perfectionism is not something you can achieve all the time, and your work doesn't have to be perfect, it just needs to be done efficiently. There is a huge difference between perfectionism and efficiency and the reason people procrastinate is because they aim for perfection over efficiency. For you to be successful you don't need to be perfect you just need to get the job done in a timely manner.

The key to living a happy life is to live a simple life. The more you complicate matters the more problems you create for yourself. You've got to come to terms with the fact that you can either do something about a problem or you can't. If you can, instead of complaining get up and do it, and if you can't it's best to let it go.

Stop Complaining

The number one habit of procrastination is complaining - the minute you break this habit you will become a better person. You are never going to have everything your way. There is always going to be a reason to complain. You just need to learn when to stop and tell yourself that it is not going to bother you anymore. Instead of worrying about a problem, it makes more sense to look at the solutions to solve that problem. While you can control certain situations, there are some that you have got to ignore and move on.

You may not be able to break all the habits of procrastination in one go. As stated previously, break tasks down and start doing it little by little until you complete everything you need to do. Don't push yourself to do things that you can't do and limit your work time to avoid burnout. Remember to take breaks in between tasks and always remind yourself that you can rather than making yourself feel bad about your work. Don't underestimate yourself, because that is one of the reasons you may start procrastinating again. No matter what, always remind yourself that you will do better, and you will achieve what you want to if you stay focused and positive.

Chapter 5:
Turn Procrastination into Motivation

If you have a lot on your plate and you have not gotten started with your list because you believe you will never manage to get anything done no matter how hard you try, just breathe! There is no denying that people lead hectic lifestyles and they are left with very little time for themselves. While people in the past worked 8-hour shifts, nowadays people spend about 12 to 15 hours to get the job done and this drains them out mentally and physically. If you believe you are not going to finish the job that you have been assigned to do on time, then it's important for you to understand how to positively transform procrastination into motivation and use it to your benefit. Let's be honest, no one likes working overtime, and this can frustrate you and make you feel like you have no time to spend on yourself. If this is something you have been going through, then you need to understand that all you must do is keep yourself motivated and teach yourself how to cut down on the external distractions so you can get work done faster.

Let's start with simple steps and go on to how you can eventually defeat procrastination and motivate yourself to become a better, more positive, and successful person.

Unplug

The first step towards focusing on the task at hand is to unplug and eliminate all unnecessary distractions, specifically your smartphone. Keep your smartphone in a drawer and do not open the drawer until you have finished a certain number of tasks you have assigned to yourself. If you absolutely must check your phone to get in touch with people, use it for no more than two minutes during the quick breaks that you give yourself in between work time. Make it a point not to access unnecessary social media sites or chat applications - if you want to send a message to somebody just dial their number and do it the old-fashioned way for faster communication.

Clean up

It's important for you to avoid distractions and clear the physical clutter around you. If you have a clean workspace you are less likely to get distracted, which is why you should make sure that your workspace is as clean as possible. It's common for people to personalize their work desk and make it look aesthetically pleasing. While an occasional family photograph or your favorite mug is something you can keep on your office desk you may want to limit accessories that are diversions and could distract you. Instead of accessorizing your workspace try keeping motivational quotes around to constantly remind you to get back to work and finish the task at hand.

Write Down Your Distractions

The more you ponder on a distraction, the more irritating it can get, and you will not be able to get your mind off it. If something is distracting you and you are not able to get it out of your head, write it down. When something distracts you and you write it down you will realize that you have managed to eliminate these distractions one at a time more effectively. Apart from thoughts that come into your head, you should also notice the things around you that may distract you. This helps you to limit their usage or get them out of sight so that you can focus more effectively on work. If you have negative reading posters or something that's too violent, distracting or graphic, you may want to get rid of them because these will unknowingly make you feel low and make you start procrastinating because they have a negative impact on your mind. When you surround yourself with positive things you feel positive and are more likely to focus on work, but when there is negativity around you it becomes difficult for you to focus on work.

Read

It important for you to exercise your brain if you want to stop procrastinating because the more active your brain is, the less likely you are to slip into a depressive phase or feel bad about yourself. Reading is the best way to exercise your brain - you may want to do the old-fashioned way or look for a Kindle to read an eBook. The benefits of reading on paper or on a Kindle is that you rest your eyes and get away from technology. There is something about reading an actual book that makes you feel relaxed. It is also great way to fall asleep and ensure that you are properly rested at night.

Take A Walk

If there are too many thoughts going on in your head and you are unable to calm your mind or your nerves before you start working, try going for a walk. Walking helps you to relax and get out all the negative energy - your body will then feel motivated and confident to start working. You don't have to go for a long walk. Even just a 10-minute walk with deep breathing exercises can work wonders to change your mood almost instantly. You can also listen to some soothing music while you are on a walk. This will help you start focusing on positive thoughts and eliminate procrastination and convert it into motivation.

Stay Healthy

You are what you eat, so when you fill junk inside of your body your physiology automatically gets affected. People who eat junk food are more likely to be depressed and sad in comparison to people who eat healthy home-cooked meals regularly. It's important for you to eat healthily and exercise because this helps your mind sharp and gives you the mental energy required to get tasks done. It is also important for you to sleep for a minimum of eight hours every day. If you don't rest well, you won't be able to perform at work well the following day. Sometimes when people procrastinate, they find it difficult to sleep because of the number of negative thoughts that fill up their head. If you want to rest well and get rid of these thoughts, then you may want to try meditation. If you meditate for a while before you head to bed each day you will manage to sleep more comfortably and be well rested for the following day.

Get Comfortable

If the office environment is too cold or too hot it may affect your productivity. If you notice that you have a lack of focus, then something you can do is to smell a lemon. The scent of a lemon is said to help increase your focus and reduce errors, making you work more effectively. Sitting by your window can also help increase your focus.

Go Green

One of the best ways to increase creativity is to have plants around you, because plants make you feel positive and motivated and they help to improve your focus and concentration. It also makes you feel happy and prevents you from procrastinating.

Use Headphones

If you find it extremely difficult to focus on work then a smart thing for you to do would be to start listening to some soothing music through headphones while working. This helps you increase your concentration and focus a lot better.

When you're in an office environment you can't really use speakers since it will distract the others around you. Speakers don't work well in disconnecting you from the rest of the world and you can still hear external noises when a speaker is on. This doesn't happen when you've got headphones which is why it's preferred.

Meditate

Meditation can help you to relax and get out all the negative thoughts from your mind almost instantly. Meditating for a little while every day not only helps you to concentrate but it also lowers the risk of destructive thoughts. One of the best ways to motivate yourself and convert procrastination into action is to start meditating daily.

Look at Happy Things

Cute pictures and happy photographs are good for you to look at because these make you feel good.

Cut Down on Meetings

Overly frequent meetings can be unnecessary and can take up a large amount of time on planning when you can invest more of that time executing the task. If you are in an authoritative position, make it a point to avoid having too many meetings and try to use that time to do execute tasks. When you do have a meeting, you should make sure the meeting is short and concise so that it is it a productive meeting rather than one that just goes on for no reason.

Delegate Tasks When Possible

While it is important for you to work hard, it also important for you to make rational decisions and think on your feet. If you have talented people who can assist you with a job, make sure that you delegate some of your responsibilities to them so that the job can be done more effectively and on time. Instead of struggling to get something done, it always is better to have more people help you achieve the goal faster.

Clean Up Your Inbox

The reason it is important for you to clean up your inbox and sort it out is that it saves a lot of time on searching for emails. People these days depend on the internet to get jobs done and the main mode of communication is email which is why your inbox should be as neatly sorted out as possible so that you don't struggle to look for emails or threads. It is just as important for you to have a clean mailbox to work efficiently as it is important for you to have a clear mind.

Track Your Time

Make sure to keep track of how many hours you work during the day and how many breaks you take in between your work time. Doing this on a regular basis will help you to cut down the amount of time that you spend wasted on your break and increase productivity of work. Ideally, try to take no longer than a 10-minute break in an hour and work for at least three hours before you take a longer break. This will contribute in a small but significant way to help you deliver more effective results within the same timeframe.

Automate

We live in a world of technology where you can automate most things to reduce your efforts, and this is something you should take advantage of. Create an RSS feed and have a certain outline ready to be emailed so you don't have to sit and type every email that you must respond to. If you know that you are going to say the same thing to 10 people in a day, it makes sense to have a template ready and only must change a name each time you need to reply. This will save you a couple of minutes for every email you send, and you can put that time to better use.

Similar Tasks

Performing all similar tasks together will help you go from one task to the other more effectively since you are already focused on something that is similar. This will take you lesser time than it would if you had to start the task fresh. At the beginning of each day, make sure you check your task list and identify similar tasks so you can group them together and make the most of the flow you have. This also helps you to finish off these tasks more efficiently.

Limit Typing

It doesn't matter how fast you are typing, it is always faster to speak, which is why you may want to use a speed dictation software to get through most of your work. Instead of writing down most of your things, you can record as much of it as possible to save time.

You're blessed to live in an age where technology is so advanced, make the most of it and use tools that can help you speed up your task, so you get stuff done faster.

Maintain A 'Stop-Doing' List

While it is important for you to have a to-do list to make sure you get through the various things you need to do on a regular basis, it is also important for you to have a 'stop-doing' list which reminds you to eliminate certain things that you would regularly do that eat into your time. This list will continue to remind you of the things that you should avoid - each time you look at it, you will know what commonly distracts you and how you need to avoid that distraction. This is a great way to overcome your procrastination habit and turn it into motivation. While most people tend to focus on a to do list, a 'stop-doing' list is just as important.

Stop Multitasking

It's important for you to understand the priorities of your task and it get done before you move on to the second task. Although a lot of people believe multitasking can help them work better, the truth is that it drains your energy and limits your focus. When you spend time multitasking, not only do you end up not being able to be efficient in one task, but you also confuse yourself and never manage to pay full attention to a task.

Try the Must, Should, Want Method

This method helps you to identify important tasks and your immediate and long-term goals that you need to complete. This is something that you should do daily and work towards achieving all three goals by prioritizing them based on importance. The must-do tasks are the ones that are most important, should-do tasks are ones you need to focus on, and the wants are the tasks that help you get closer to your long-term goals but that you should focus on last.

Avoid Checking Emails on Your Commute

Checking emails is a high priority task but this isn't something you should be doing on your commute because you invest double the amount of time checking your emails when you reach work. You end up double checking them again when you want to reply. Instead, give yourself enough time to go to your inbox when you are settled down at work so you can reply to them the same time you read them, saving on the time you invested initially opening and reading through each mail. This also lowers the risk of losing an important mail or missing out on one because you forgot to mark it unread it after checking it.

Do That "One Thing"

Ask yourself what is most important and make sure that you get that one thing done effectively. Try to ask yourself every day about the one thing that you want to get done during that day and make sure that you do it first.

Choose Your Important Task Wisely

Look at the list of tasks that you have and pick the most important first, so you get it done at a time when you are most energetic and when you are most focused. You can choose to write the tasks on a sheet of paper and stick it to your computer screen or somewhere where you can look at it over and over again, so you keep reminding yourself that this task is pending. It's important for you to remind yourself because not only does this motivate you to work a little harder but it ensures that you don't forget about it.

Start with Creative Work

It is important for you to focus on creative tasks and get them finished first because that's when your brain is fresh, and you can think better. Always try to finish tasks that require your mind to focus more effectively faster than leave it for the second half of the day when you are mentally drained out. Your creative tasks turn out to be better when they are done with a fresh mind and you also end up in investing leisure time doing it.

Be Picky

It's essential for you to be picky about the kind of work you choose because if you end up doing almost anything and everything that comes your way, you burden yourself with too much work and you will not be able to handle it as effectively as you would like to. While it is important to stay busy and have a full work day it's not recommended to bite off more than you can chew because this will affect the overall quality of your work. If you have a clear mindset, you will end up choosing the kind of work you want to accept and pick the things that you know you will be able to complete effectively and confidently. Instead of comparing how much money a task will make, try to ask you yourself how effectively you will be able to complete these tasks.

Plan Your To-Do List the Night Before

It is very important to have a to-do list on a regular basis. The best way to make the most out of your to-do list is to plan the night before. You will have a clear idea of what your following day looks like and how well you will be able to handle the tasks that you have planned for the day. This habit saves you time of having to sit down and make a to do list at the start of your day and enables you to put that time into doing something more fruitful.

Always Sort Tasks Based on Priority

It's important for you to sort out your tasks based on priority, focusing on ones that are most important and moving on to the ones that are less important by the end of the day. When you start your day, you are always more motivated, and you will be able to put all your energy into doing important and urgent tasks better. If something goes wrong during the day and you are not able to complete the remainder of your tasks you know for sure that you managed to finish the important ones and you only missed out on the ones that were not so important or not so urgent.

Always Ask Yourself Five Questions:

- Does the solution help you get closer to your goal?
- Is it important to your employer/your boss?
- Does it help you earn good money?
- Does it make your life easier?
- Do you need to complete it urgently?

When you have the answer to these questions not only will you be able to prioritize effectively but you will manage to eliminate the tasks that are not so important, and it will help plan your day to deliver better results.

Break Down Your Tasks into Subtasks

As we had discussed before, you need to break down your tasks into smaller portions so that you are able to deal with them effectively. When breaking down the tasks try to focus on creating sub-tasks that are no longer than 30 minutes each because this will allow you to put in more effort into completing the task and you'll also stay focused and achieve better results. When you break your tasks into 30-minute sub tasks, you end up doing them more effectively.

The Two-Minute Rule

If there are small tasks on your plate that will require less than 2 minutes to complete, give yourself a certain amount of time to finish as many of those tasks as possible. This will help you to increase your motivation, and in case you are having a bad day, or you are not available you would have still managed to get quite a lot of your tasks done by simply focusing on the smaller ones.

Eat the Frog

The big tasks are usually the ones you dread most, so focus on breaking it down into small pieces try to complete as much of the tasks as possible when you are still fresh. This will help you overcome procrastination and motivate yourself. It's always recommended to start off with the tougher tasks so you can get done with it early in the day. If you can't manage to look at a tough task, break it down!

When you look at a big task, you tend to feel less motivated to begin working on it, but the minute you break it down into smaller ones you get going and manage to complete it in a short time span. This helps you increase productivity without stressing about big tasks and increases efficiency.

Find Your Biological Prime Time

Everyone has a "prime time" - a magical time where you are most motivated, or you can get a maximum amount of work done. When you are in this zone, you try to put in as much energy as you can to do work because it's the time when you will be good at what you do, and your productivity will be at its peak.

Visible Progress

It's important for you to be able to monitor and measure your progress because this will help you figure out how well you are doing, and it continues to motivate you to push harder. If you don't see results, it's difficult for you to continue your work and this will push you back instead of motivating you to move forward.

Don't Break the Chain

Make it a point to set goals for yourself every day and continue finding your rhythm without breaking the chain. There are going to be external factors from time to time that may affect the way you think or make you feel a little low, but your focus should be to remember to stick to your plan.

Start Challenging Yourself

Time yourself every week and see how long it takes you to complete a task. Start challenging yourself to complete them in shorter time spans but in realistic time frames. Give yourself a small reward every time you achieve something - treating yourself when you achieve a goal makes you feel good and this helps to enhance your productivity. It's important to stay in a good mood and constantly motivate yourself towards getting better. When you have a positive attitude, you've already won half the battle!

Stay Confident

No matter what kind of job you have it is important for you to do it with confidence and believe in yourself. When you stop telling yourself that you are good at what you do, and you'll be able to complete your work effectively not only will you get better results, but you will feel motivated to do the work. Always keep a strong posture with your chin up because at the end of the day your posture matters and your confidence will increase.

Be Happy

The most important way you will be able to increase your productivity is when you are happy. Do little things every day to put a smile on your face because this not only makes you feel better, but it eliminates procrastination and diverts your mind towards motivation.

These little changes may not seem like a lot but when you incorporate them and begin enjoying your life, not only will you benefit from them, but you'll also manage to successfully transform your procrastination into motivating yourself to do better each day.

Chapter 6:
Time Management Strategies by Millionaires

It's no secret that millionaires have made choices which have led them on the path of success. Therefore, they become role models for almost everyone. If you want to think like a millionaire, it's important for you to use their time and management secrets so you learn how to balance your day more effectively and understand what choices need to be made and how to make the right decisions when it matters most. There is no denying that a millionaire has a better sense of time management as compared to other people and they understand exactly what to do with the time and how to use it most effectively. Considering they need to deal with at least a thousand emails a day, they also need to figure out how they are going to communicate effectively with their employees and schedule meetings to organize strategies for their work. Successful people simply make the right decisions because it is necessary to make informed decisions to help the team get on the path of success. Here are some interesting facts about millionaires that you should keep in mind:

Most millionaires wake up early in the morning because they like to spend time with their families. They understand how important it is to maintain a work/life balance and they do what it takes to make the most of the time they have. This includes waking up early to prepare breakfast for their kids just to see them smile!

They always find time to exercise because fitness is important and with a healthy body comes a healthy mind, which helps them to focus on work better. While some people always find an excuse to not exercise, a millionaire is usually looking for ways to fit in a workout even if it's just for 15 minutes. They like working out regularly because it gives them more energy and helps them to cope with tough days and balance out energy when they need it.

They pay a lot of attention to reading because it helps them to learn more information and it helps to exercise the brain regularly. Apart from physical exercise, millionaires also make it a point to read regularly so they can exercise their brain and learn new things. Even after they have accomplished most of what they had set out to do, they continue challenging themselves every day!

Eliminate Time Spent in Meetings

Several businesses often believe that investing unnecessary time in a meeting is not going to benefit them. You need to figure out what's important and what isn't for your business so you can profit from it more effectively. Instead of wasting time talking to your employees regarding what needs to be done, it makes more sense to just let them do the work. When less time is spent in meetings you can spend more time getting the job done rather than discussing how it needs to be done. Take note of tasks that you believe are unnecessary and eliminate them from the workspace completely. Use automated tools and shared drives that make it easier for your employees to coordinate with one another so that can you get more effective results out of them and so they end up working at higher efficiency levels.

If you absolutely must have a meeting with your employees, have a meeting that is no longer than 10 minutes. Make sure to cover up everything you want to convey in the meeting in clear communication and then get that employee to communicate to others. Meetings don't need to be long. So, don't let a meeting last too long where employees will end up getting demotivated. Have a quick meeting discussing important aspects of the work and carry on getting the job done.

Start Your Day with A Bang

It is important for you to use your energy to complete tasks that matter, and this is exactly what all millionaires do as well. While people have a misconception that they should have meetings at the start of the day, the truth is, meetings are not a priority and they can be left for the end of the day just before the employees leave so that people know what they need to do starting the following day. The more important the task, the better it is to get it done in the earlier part of your day because you have a lower chance of distraction and distractions are also fewer in comparison to when you have an office full of people constantly asking you to do things.

Have Themed Days

It's important for you to raise the motivation levels of your employees so you should always plan different kinds of themes from time to time in the organization. It can be difficult if you must work too many hours a day, but if you learn how to delegate your work effectively you will be able to be more productive and get more out of your employees than expected. Themed days help to keep your employees in control and makes them very disciplined which is essential to accomplish success. It takes over distractions and it ensures that the employees understand the importance of getting the job done on time. Some theme examples include:

- Mondays for management
- Tuesdays for product
- Wednesdays for marketing
- Thursdays for partnership
- Fridays for culture
- Saturdays for holiday
- Sundays for reflection and preparation for Monday

Discipline Is Essential

It's very important to keep motivation levels high in your organization but you also need to maintain a certain level of discipline if you want your employees to be productive. Hiring a team of intelligent employees aren't going to benefit you if they are not productive. The only way they will be able to be productive is when they have discipline and they follow the rules. When you have a team of people not only look for smart ones but look for the ones who are disciplined because this will manage to improve your business. The kind of employees you hire at the end of the day will help to build your business or destroy it completely.

Recharge and Refresh Midday

If you are going to continue working for long periods of time, don't do that without a break as it's not going to benefit you. You should yourself a break in between so that you can continue to work at the same pace you started off with during the day. This is one of the main reasons why it's important to break down the tasks at hand and give yourself breaks in between so that you manage to do it effectively rather than stress about completing the whole thing in one go. Millionaires tend to take shorter breaks during the day, so they keep motivation levels high and have the same amount of energy that they did at the start of the day right until the end. This helps them to deliver quality work from start to finish. The little breaks you take will benefit you in the long run because you never feel overwhelmed.

Focus on Creating Good Product Rather Than Making Money

If you want to stay in business long-term you must provide quality services and products because that's what will help you make money automatically. Your main motive shouldn't be to make money but rather to create products that will satisfy customers and will be available to them at an affordable price. Continue to think about innovative products and interesting ways you will be able to better your product every day.

Let this be your motivation to move forward and let it encourage you to do something that you know is good. This helps to foster a feel-good factor which automatically increases the amount of work you do and the quality of the work too. Remember, when you are a business owner you create job opportunities and there are a lot of people who depend on your business. Not only should you focus on growing your business for your benefit but also for the benefit of the employees who work under your wing. When you consider their success as yours not only does your business grow more effectively but it also makes you feel good and that motivates you to get to work every day and do better.

Learn to Give Yourself More Time

When you are in the middle of a busy work schedule, the one thing that you need to remember is to give yourself enough me time so that you can relax and resume work again before you are burdened with more tasks to do. During your 'do not disturb' time, all you need to do is relax and let go of all the planning in your head so that you can prepare yourself for the following tasks. No matter how busy you are, you should always find time to relax during a tough day at work because this helps you to focus better and realize what you could do better. If you constantly bury yourself in work without giving yourself a break, you will experience burn out.

Chapter 7:
The Secret to Building Self-Discipline

In order for you to overcome procrastination, you need to have strong self-discipline, so you don't allow yourself to get tempted every step you take. While you don't expect yourself to improve yourself instantly, it's a learning process and every step you take can help you get closer to your desired goal. There are many things that you can do in order to build your self-discipline and stay strong but here are some effective secrets that are known to work.

Know Your Weaknesses

The first stage of getting self-discipline in place is to recognize your weaknesses and accept that you have some. Everyone wants to believe that they are strong, and they don't have any weakness, but the truth is that there are many things that could be a weakness for you and in order to get better you got to overcome weaknesses effectively and turn it into your strengths.

The first step is to confront the weaknesses you have so that you can identify them effectively and understand exactly how to deal with it.

There are solutions for every weakness, and they can easily be converted into strengths with a little effort. This is something you must continuously remind yourself about because if you don't acknowledge your weakness you will never be able to deal with it in the first place.

If you don't manage to recognize your weaknesses on your own, you can always consult people you trust and ask them to help you out. You need to be prepared to face a few critiques you may not like but that is part of the process of learning and becoming self-disciplined. Once you identify your weakness it is easier for you to learn how to withstand it and fight it in a more streamlined manner.

Your weakness doesn't necessarily have to be a distraction or a flaw that you give into, it could also be something at work or a task you may not be good at.

You need to prepare yourself to hear the truth about the various kinds of tasks that you can and can't you do so that you know how to deal with them and you do not waste time on attempting something you may not manage to get done as effectively as you would like to.

If your weakness lies at work and there is a portion of a task you can't get done and it haunts you every time you get to it, give it to somebody who may be good at it.

When you ask somebody to get the work that you are not good at done, you maintain consistency in your work, and you know for a fact that you will be able to get it completed on time without procrastination in the process. When you come across something you are weak at, there is a chance that you give into temptation and deviate from the task at hand. This could cause you to end up losing focus but when you hand it over to somebody else you can continue working at a steady pace without reaching a breaking point during your work schedule. You also need to remember not to stress about perfection because that's one of the major problems of procrastinating and if you want everything to be perfect you will never manage to finish a task on time.

Attempt to try different ways to solve the problem. A wise entrepreneur once said that aggregation is the mother of invention, so if you don't have the skills try again with a different approach. Try to learn how others manage to deal with it and see if you can get some insights on converting that weakness of yours into a strength.

Remove Temptations

Temptations are something that waste your time and make you procrastinate because people end up postponing a job that needs to be done so they can indulge in a temptation. While some people have more control over temptation than others, giving in to temptation at the wrong time will often make some of the temptations turn into obsessions and when this happens, your productivity decreases drastically. Due to this you won't be able to figure out how you can self-discipline yourself again. If you want to make sure you don't give in to temptation you need to learn how to deal with it tactfully and learn how to say no at the right times.

The first stage is to identify a potential temptation and learn how to control the temptation, not just temporarily, but permanently and for the long-term. Whether it is the urge to get up from your work desk and go smoke or whether it is to delay an important project, you need to learn what interferes with your long-term goal and how you can stay focused. Binge eating and smoking is bad for health and it will make you feel low and guilty after you have given into the temptation. If your temptations are high, you may want to ask people to help you to control it. If you are a smoker and you do not want to smoke in between your project, then try to keep your pack of cigarettes away from you and promise yourself not to touch it until you have finished your task at hand. Similarly, if you are craving to binge eat then you can replace your unhealthy option with a healthy snack so that you don't feel bad about snacking. The kind of food you eat can help increase or decrease your productivity so make your choices wisely.

Learn to remove yourself from temptation in the long run. If you crave to smoke a cigarette and you are trying to quit, make sure that you get rid of anything and everything that reminds you of smoking, so it gets easier for you not to give in to the temptation. You must remember that temptation takes a while to get over completely so don't force yourself into a situation where it affects your productivity but rather try to control it little by little until you achieve your desired goal. Remember, when there is something that tempts you, try to tell yourself that there is also a solution to the problem that may be better for you rather than giving in to the temptation because this will help to self-discipline yourself more effectively.

Be honest with yourself because if you keep lying to yourself and giving into temptation, it won't help you progress. One of the first things you need to do is be honest because if you cheat and lie to people about not giving into temptation when you do, you will start feeling guilty and this will affect your productivity more than you would have expected.

If your urge to give in to a temptation increases drastically, imagine yourself resisting it in your head. A visual interpretation of rejecting something can make you stronger and believe that you can achieve it. You need to work towards building a strong resistance against temptation if you want to handle it effectively.

Whenever you have the urge to give in to a temptation, try to think about the consequences the temptation will eventually lead to. Whether it is wasting time instead of focusing on work, giving in to the urge of smoking, or even binging on unhealthy food it's not going to do you any good, so you need to realize that the sooner you learn how to resist this temptation, the more fruitful and successful your life will become. Remind yourself of all the bad things the temptations can eventually lead to and this will help you to stay strong. If the temptation becomes really bad, then you may want to try distracting yourself for a bit so that the temptation passes by. Sometimes simply closing your eyes and meditating for a few minutes can help you overcome the strongest of temptations and make you feel good about yourself and get you back on track at work. This technique works well with smokers who constantly crave smoking and are trying to give up. When you are faced with temptation but overcome those first few minutes, you'll be able to resist and be strong on your path of self-discipline.

You need to have a mindset that tells you firmly you will not give in no matter what and that this is a stepping stone towards becoming more self-disciplined in life.

Set Clear Goals and Have an Execution Plan

One of the best ways to become more self-disciplined is to set goals for yourself. These goals don't necessarily need to revolve around your work and they can be anything from something as simple as making sure that you get up at a particular time every day and head to bed at a particular time, or more challenging, for example, eating healthy food at least five days a week and exercising for a few minutes every day. When you plan your goals, you need to plan them in a realistic manner so that you don't slip and fall back into old habits because you are too hard on yourself. Avoid setting goals that are too difficult to achieve as you may end up disappointing yourself and losing interest in the goal completely.

While you should always aim very high you need to start low and keep celebrating in between so that you're motivated to go on. There are different ways to set goals for yourself - if you want to set a goal to help you focus better at work you can create a chart that tells you what must be done at each hour of the day and aim towards achieving it. If you want to overcome your temptations, then setting goals is a great way to do this because it helps you to become more self-disciplined and you'll train your mind to do the right thing.

For a lot of people their cell phones are a huge distraction during the day and one of the best ways to deal with this is to set a goal of not touching your phone at hours unless you need to make an important phone call.

Scrolling through your social media platforms and seeing what others are up to is not going to get you anywhere, so you need to train your mind to stay off social media platforms when you are focusing and work more efficiently. That's a goal you should aim to achieve every day. Give yourself short breaks in between your work schedule and allow yourself to indulge in your social media addiction for a few minutes during that break. If you fail to keep up to your goal and you still go and check these applications on your phone in between your work schedule, penalize yourself by not doing it for the rest of the day. When you start training yourself to focus and be more productive not only do you incorporate self-discipline, but you also become more effective in what you do. You will realize that by eliminating small temptations not only do you end up performing better but you get more time for yourself that you can utilize to do more productive work. If you want to be successful you need to put the maximum time into working and focus at achieving your goals both in the long-term and short-term on a regular basis. While long-term goals are essential, it is also important for you to have short-term goals because these can eventually lead you to your long-term goal. Just like with a big task that you break down into multiple smaller tasks to make it easier, you need to do the same with your goals so that you can achieve it a little at a time.

Many times, people ask other people to help set goals for them. This is something you should avoid completely because when another person sets the goal for you, you don't feel as motivated towards working on the goal as you would when you set one yourself. They also don't know your limits which means you can either end up with a goal that is too simple to achieve or one that's extremely difficult.

You also need to be clear about what your success looks like so that you can aim high and working hard towards achieving it. Always have a plan in place so you don't go astray, and you learn how to self-discipline yourself one step at a time. You get to value the importance of your goals because your goal is your end target, and this is what will keep you motivated towards doing better and understanding the importance of self-discipline in your life.

Focus your eyes on the prize; this is something that will keep you positive even on the lowest of days. If you want to achieve your goal on time you have to track your performance to make sure you don't slip away from the final target and that you work hard every day towards achieving it.

Build Your Self-Discipline

Self-discipline isn't something that you were born with. For you to become a self-disciplined person you need to work hard. There are various things that you can do in order to achieve self-discipline but teaching it to yourself one step at a time works in your favor. Make sure you understand what your goal is before you start self-disciplining yourself because self-discipline works on the principle of controlling a certain situation. You need to identify what that situation is for you to discipline yourself. Find out the reasons why because it's important for you to know them. A good reason for self-discipline is that it is the fuel that helps you pump in more energy into focusing and inspiring yourself every day of your life. Keep asking yourself what you want to do, how you want to do it, and why you want to do it, and once you have gotten the answers for this, constantly remind yourself that these are the reasons you want to teach yourself self-discipline. Self-discipline does require a lot of commitment and accountability which means it is likely you may be diverted into thoughts that are unnecessary. You must hold yourself accountable for every action you make, so make sure you understand why you have done it so that you are able to control the situation.

If you want to instill this in yourself, you need to remind yourself that you cannot blame others for the choices you make and that no matter what situation you are in it's important to identify how you are going to deal with it in an effective manner. While it is good to reward yourself for something that you have done well, it is also needed that you penalize yourself when you do something wrong. When you correct yourself for a mistake you committed or a slip up you had, it helps you to not repeat the same mistake again and encourages you to do better. Everyone has temptations but learning to deal with them in an effective way is what self-discipline is all about. The sooner you understand what you need to do versus what you want to do and figure out which is more important, you will be able to master the skill of self-discipline.

You hold yourself accountable for your self-discipline skills so it's up to you to decide what level of self-discipline you want to set for yourself. You can choose to be extremely hard on yourself or give yourself a little leverage depending on your goal and the number of temptations or distractions you have in life. You need to ask yourself various questions and determine where you stand before you decide the standard of self-discipline you want to incorporate in your life. Forcing yourself to lead a very reclusive life when you are a social person may be difficult and something that is unrealistic for you to achieve. It would be better for you to aim at choosing a simple yet effective technique that allows you to indulge in a little temptation every now and then so you can get back to focusing on your tasks.

Create New Habits

There are various things that you can do in order to focus on self-discipline but the most important is to create a habit that you can work with and use it to your benefit.

It's important for you to know that you can be motivated with what is important to you. You need to understand that your goal is not to watch the motivation happen but rather the commitment towards the task and getting it done on time which is why you need commitment rather than motivation. One of the most important things for you is to be committed long-term towards getting your job done regularly without the distractions of any other temptations. You should be disciplined and continue working even on days where you don't feel motivated.

You also need to understand that when you get a job done you should not just look at the results but rather how much you know about the task so that you can deliver quality of work. It's very important for you to focus on being positive because without good quality you will never be able to deliver the results that you want. As I stated above, if you find it difficult to get a certain portion of your task completed because you lack the skills, you need to work towards building on that skill rather than getting frustrated.

Make it an exciting and fun journey when you work because this will make you work more effectively, and it will help you enjoy what you do every day of your life. The one thing you should remember is to always be happy with the task you have in hand because it will make you feel satisfied. You need to try and get rid of negative feelings because these negative feelings will hold you back and it will leave you stagnant in a profession. When you teach yourself self-discipline, the one thing that you need to remember is to encourage yourself to do better and not stagnate in one place for very long. If you want to achieve success, you must constantly move ahead and make better choices in life to improve on the life you live. This will happen if you are happy with the kind of work you do. You can learn to enjoy your work in an effective way so that you spend most of your time doing it rather than procrastinating. You should also use your imagination and focus on the positive attributes of life that make you feel happy instead of thinking negative thoughts that will pull down your energy. If you want to challenge yourself, you should do it because this will force you to do something and when you do it with a smile on your face you will enjoy everything you do towards getting closer to success.

Not only will you manage to become better at self-discipline, but you will also get better at the kind of work you deliver, bringing you closer towards success. When you want to motivate yourself every now and then you should push yourself when necessary. If you really want to do something you need to challenge yourself and commit to learning how to get it done the right way. If you have been given a task, break it up into parts and see if you can get it done on your own. If you can't delegate, then try to figure out the way to learn this task one bit at a time because then you no longer must depend on someone to get your job done.

The more you challenge yourself, the better you will get because you start teaching yourself by practicing more and this works out in your favor in the long run.

You might be wondering if your current path will make you successful or not. Using motivational words or phrases multiple times a day will make you believe in your ability. You also need to watch what you eat because the truth is, the kind of food you eat helps you to either increase your productivity and this also determines how successful you will be eventually.

There are several food items that help you feel positive while there are some that can make you feel low and negative and increase procrastination. If you want to be successful, not only do you need to self-discipline yourself but also change the kind of food that you eat. Eating junk food is something that will ruin your system and will encourage medical problems such as hormonal imbalance and thyroid issues that make you slower and more lethargic, thereby limiting your ability to work to your full potential. Similarly, when you eat healthy meals at regular intervals your energy levels are always high, and you will be able to get the job done without any distractions.

One of the best ways to eat healthy is to eat home-cooked meals that are not prepared using too much oil and give you a complete balanced diet which includes green vegetables as well as your required protein. It may surprise you that the color of fruit also has a huge impact on your life and fruits that are fresh and come in different colors, especially the bright ones, will make you feel happy and lift your spirits. One of the best ways to stay successful is to start eating healthy and fresh meals because fresh food manages to make you feel fit almost instantly.

While several people depend on caffeine to keep their energy levels high and help them to focus through a tough day at work, this might not be a good solution for you as it interferes with your ability to think. It is also known to cause sleep deprivation, so if you have a cup of coffee a little later in the day you may struggle to fall asleep. This will affect your following day and make you feel tired and drowsy and this will hamper your ability to work effectively. Self-discipline is important because it will help you plan to eat regularly and when you eat your meals on time you will provide your body with the proper nutrients that make you healthier. If you want to be successful you need to look after your health, and it all begins with what you eat.

If you're eating habits are bad and you end up eating at wrong times of the day, the smart thing for you to do would be to stock up on healthy snacks including fruits that you can eat even while you are working. Not only does this help keep your energy levels up but it also helps you feel full and happy. When you remain hungry, the irritability begins, and you will not be able to stay as focused on your job as you would with a full stomach.

When looking to follow a healthy diet you should remember that moderation is very important and if you start to eat too much of one thing it is not going to benefit you in any way. Focusing only on eating salads will not give you the amount of energy you need to go through the day which means you have to get your fair share of protein as well. Take your time to craft out a diet plan that gives you all the essential nutrients you need in order to keep you energized. Some people also choose to take a multivitamin at the start of the day - while it is not necessary, you could pick one up at a local drug store. While some people are against the thought of using a multivitamin, it is good for you because it provides the body with all the necessary nutrients that you need.

How you eat also matters because some people don't really care about where they sit while eating or how fast they end up eating their food. Some people turn on the television and start eating larger meals because they want to go through the entire television series or program that they started watching while eating. If the program is soon going to end, they end up chewing their food a lot faster and this does not foster healthy digestion. If you want your digestive system to work properly you must chew your food well so that you digest it and boost your metabolism levels. High metabolism levels mean more energy and the ability to get more done during the day.

It is important for you to work at your full potential and eating a healthy meal is one of the habits you may have to get used to before you adapt to it completely.

Change Your Perception About Willpower

If you want to accomplish something, it is important for you to set the right habits and make self-discipline a part of your regular routine so that you don't have to prepare yourself every day to stay focused and get the job done correctly. This is not going to happen immediately, and it would require a lot of willpower for you to make this possible. The habits that you have are usually formed because of a routine that you were used to following and it's not going to break the minute you decide you no longer benefit from a habit. Unfortunately, losing the bad habit may be more difficult than changing good habits so you must make sure that you figure out how you will start changing to get habituated to the right things.

When you build good habits, it helps you to conserve a lot of resources and put them to use effectively and this helps you to save energy when needed the most. It helps you to relax in stressful situations and overcome anxiety problems so that you don't worry about whether you will be able to get through the day or not.

Habits are formed in the brain, which means getting rid of a habit is difficult and instead of training yourself to overcome a habit you need to start training yourself to introducing habits that work well for you. Give yourself time to train your brain to develop healthy habits that incorporate self-discipline in your life, and this will benefit you in the long run. Rome wasn't built in a day and good habits won't come to you instantly either. It's a struggle and you must give up a lot of old habits and form new ones that help you to stay strong and increase willpower. The best way to overcome bad habits is to learn to say no and not give into temptation little by little. No matter what you are dealing with, always try to approach the situation one step at a time because it makes the journey that much easier.

When you are planning to set a good habit or a good example for yourself, you need to remember that you can't just stray from the actual goal because this is what matters most. You need to have a healthy routine to follow but not make it something you will be paranoid about or must put all your energy into. It's a small change you need to make on a regular basis, so you get used to it and become part of your routine life. This helps to incorporate self-discipline long-term and more effectively.

Give Yourself A Backup Plan

Backup plans are smaller agreements that you can keep going back to and altering to suit your preference. A lot of people believe that it's important to have a backup plan in order to become successful so that if you fail at plan A, you can immediately switch to plan B. This may seem really efficient and low-risk which is why it's so popular, but the truth is having a plan can not only increase the chances of procrastination, but it also diverts your mind from self-discipline because you always know you have a plan B to depend on.

If you want to be successful, the number one thing you need to do is keep yourself off the leverage of being able to switch to another plan and believe that this is your only option. People who usually switch to plan B tend to mess up the second plan as well because they won't able to focus on it and get it done the first time and chances that they will mess it up again are quite high.

When you have a plan B you tend to take plan A lightly, and this does not work well for your success rate which is why you must think about your initial plan as the only option to work with if you want to succeed. The reason you choose plan A to begin with is because you believe it's the right way to go about a situation, so don't second doubt yourself.

Forgive Yourself and Move Forward

We are all human, and this means that there will be times when we end up making mistakes. Sometimes these mistakes are a little more severe than we would imagine, and this often leads us to get upset about the situation. Things may not always work out the way you planned, and while it's not good to have a plan B, you need to start fresh instead of not being able to move on. Forgiveness is important for you to move on and without forgiving yourself you will not be able to take the next step ahead. There are various stages to forgiveness and if you want to start anew then you must go through all the stages so that you do not repeat the same mistake. The first stage of forgiveness begins with responsibility. You need to take responsibility for the wrong that you have done so you can work your way up the ladder towards the other stages. Sometimes people procrastinate at the first stage and they refuse to accept that they have made a mistake. Once you admit that you are at fault, you then need to work towards the second stage which is remorse.

You need to feel remorse for the situation you put yourself in and all your coworkers or friends for that matter and feel bad about it. Unless you feel bad about a mistake you made, you will not be able to correct it so you need to bring yourself to this stage and by taking responsibility before you are ready to move to the third stage. The third stage of forgiveness is restoration. This is where you begin to plan your tasks all over again and do it with confidence so that you will not fail. Once you are on this stage you can then begin executing your plan and go towards the final stage of renewal. It's important for you to understand and forgive yourself for the mistakes you have made and moving on without holding any guilt or bad taste regarding the experience. Self-discipline is also about controlling the way you feel about your emotions. If you want to be successful and you want to make the most out of your life you must learn to get ahold of your emotions, so you are able to deal with the most complex situations with finesse.

Chapter 8:
Essential Phrases to Stop Procrastinating

There are six P's that you need to keep in mind that will help you avoid procrastination: Prior Planning Prevents Piss Poor Performance. These 6 Ps are the key to ensuring that you plan well in advance and take care of performance issues.

Prior Planning Prevents Piss Poor Performance

These are the 6 P's that you need to keep in mind when you want to avoid procrastination. Planning is the key element to making sure that you get tasks completed on time. If you want to make sure that you are finishing a task within a given time frame, then you need to start planning well in advance. When you are given a task at work and you need to complete that within the next couple of days, it makes more sense to start taking care of the task the very same day that you receive it. Putting it on the back burner and waiting until the very last day will not help you deliver quality performance. Often, procrastination leads to extremely poor performance and this is what the 6 P's will tell you. When you plan and strategize well in advance you will eliminate the possibility of poor performance.

Physically Preparing for Things

There are several things that you may be mentally prepared to do, however, when the time comes to go ahead and do it, it becomes difficult. One classic example is planning to go to the gym. Everyone has done this at least once in their lifetime. You end up spending money on an expensive gym membership and you do not have the motivation to head to the gym. This is where physical preparation will help you. If you know that you must head to the gym at 6:00 in the morning, then you should try and sleep in your gym clothes. As silly as this may sound, it is actually a very helpful exercise because when you wake up you will already be physically prepared to go to the gym and there will be no excuse left for you. If you decide not to go to the gym, then you will have to change and get into your home clothes. The task of having to change early in the morning can deter you from changing and it will motivate you to head to the gym. When you physically prepare, it makes it very easy for you to go ahead and complete your task.

Try and Visualize Your Problems

When you start visualizing your problems you will start fearing the consequences and this will push you towards completing your task. Have you ever noticed that you are anxious to complete your tasks on time when there is a fear of your boss standing over you? These are the kind of consequences that you need to visualize, and this will help you face your problems and complete tasks without having to procrastinate.

Plan for Tomorrow

When you start your day, you need to make sure that you plan. When you do not have a plan in place, your brain will not know which direction to head towards and this will leave you wandering without any purpose for the day. You need to make sure that you plan everything well in advance and this will help your brain plans various activities. This can be seen in the example of studying for an exam. If you know that you have a science exam the next day, you should create a plan that will help you cover certain topics as soon as you wake up. This will help your brain to be mentally prepared and you will be able to prepare well for the exam.

Chapter 9:
The 5-Second Rule Mind Hack

When it comes to working towards success and doing things that can help you improve your lifestyle and get closer to your goals, the 5-second rule comes in handy. There are a lot of reasons why this rule works, and one of them is that it's not time-consuming. As the name suggests, it is a 5-second rule and it needs to be acted upon within 5 seconds of the conception of the idea so that your brain doesn't shun the idea completely. This concept was designed by Mel Robbins, and according to Mel, if you have an intuitive desire to work on a goal or accomplish something you need to physically move and initiate action by the end of the fifth second without wasting any more time. All you have is a 5-second window where you have an extremely high motivation level and you will be able to make the decision right there and then without any change of plans.

With the 5-second rule, you need to remember that there are five elements in it and each element is equally important. The process begins with you counting backwards from 5 to 1. This begins with the first second, and this is the moment when you have an instinct. When we talk about an instinct, it needs to be a healthy, positive one and not something that will affect your mindset or your lifestyle negatively. If you have the urge to go buy an expensive cell phone, that is not a positive instinct. However, if you suddenly realize that there is an interesting topic you want to start writing about because you believe it's going to be a bestseller you need to start working on it within 5-seconds so that the bubbles of wisdom inside of you start creating an ocean of knowledge that you can start flowing out of your system. The minute you have an impulse or an instinct to do something you need to act upon it almost instantly, and this is where the second element comes in. The second element is to act on the goal; this is crucial because you need to make sure this is a choice of getting up and walking towards doing what you believe is really going to be effective in your life. If you decide that you want to write a book and you already selected the topic then the second goal is achieved. We often refer to the 5-second rule as a gut feeling and a feeling that we often ignore believing it's just a passing phase. What we don't realize is this feeling can sometimes help you succeed more effectively than any other plans ever will.

After you decide you want to go ahead with the goal, you come to the third element - this is to push yourself to go ahead and act. Once you have decided and as soon as you know that it's right, you must push yourself, establish from ground level, and build on the idea of writing your book. This is where you take control of the situation and decide what needs to be done for you to move ahead with this decision of yours. You just need to picture what you believe you want to do and then move on to the next element which is to move within the next 5 seconds.

This may seem very complicated to you and you may be wondering how you can accomplish all of this within 5 seconds. You don't have to! Every element in Mel Robbins' book requires 5 seconds for you to decide and that's the reason it is called the 5-second rule. From the minute the idea was conceived in your brain you need to give yourself 5 seconds to feel in your heart that your decision is the right decision and you are not going to fail when you go ahead with the plan. If you get a positive feeling about the idea it is something worth moving on with and you go to your final element which is to act, or your brain will forget about it. This is where you either pick up the phone and let somebody know what you are doing or note it down on a piece of paper so that you remind yourself that you plan to do this. If somebody comes up with multiple of these ideas in a day but the 5-second window destroys the ideas, those ideas aren't fruitful and not important. Subconsciously we have multiple such ideas throughout the day but only a few sticks out and these are the ones you need to look out for.

If you want the 5-second rule to prove beneficial to you, it is important for you to start living a lifestyle that is healthy and to self-discipline yourself. It's not easy to think positive thoughts when you have a negative mindset - a negative and emotional person will not be able to work towards the path of success confidently. Procrastination is one of the leading causes of failure and if you want to become successful you need to take your first step towards overcoming procrastination and making yourself a stronger and more successful person one step at a time. This is not a difficult choice to make. It is something you can do very effectively when you put your mind to it. Whether it is changing your bad habits or incorporating the 5-second rule, the minute you learn how to challenge yourself you will start to see change and this change would be for the better.

Chapter 10: The Japanese Technique to Overcome Laziness

Almost everyone has had a goal in their life only to realize that they were heading towards failure after a few weeks or months. If you want to challenge yourself and overcome laziness then it's important for you to accept that although you are not ready, you need to push yourself to do it now and not tomorrow or next week. While you always start off something with a lot of motivation it will eventually end up fading out and we lose interest in the goal that we planned to set out to achieve. One of the major reasons this happens is because we try to achieve too much too fast and the new responsibilities that we have taken up don't work well to help us change our old habits and adjust to the new ones.

One of the reasons why it's important for you to understand how essential it is to incorporate change one step at a time is because this helps you to achieve success and no matter how long it takes to you to train your body, it is always going to be worth it. If you want to overcome procrastination, then the Japanese technique for overcoming laziness is something you may want to try out. This method is known as Kaizen, also referred to as the one-minute principle.

So, what does this one-minute principal teach you and how does it work? In Japanese culture, the practice of Kaizen is a one-minute self-improvement principle you need to teach yourself. The center of this principle is an idea or a goal that you want to set for yourself to do. Start practicing this for 1 minute at the same time every day. This won't be difficult for anybody to do and it will make it convenient for you to incorporate this into your life with no hassle. People find it very difficult to take out 15 minutes or 30 minutes of the day but one minute will unlikely have any effect on your life.

Whether you decide to read or listen to a podcast, do it for 1 minute every day. When you begin doing this activity you may not enjoy it and you may even regret making this decision in the first place. After a few days you will realize that this seemingly unpleasant activity has started to bring you a lot of satisfaction and happiness so much that you look forward to it. The one minute you invested every day is something that you start taking seriously and this helps you to slowly but surely move towards self-discipline and this helps you to achieve better results.

When you overcome the lack of confidence, feelings of guilts or the belief that you will not be able to do something, you start moving towards a successful path and move forward. Inspiring yourself is important if you want to stay away from procrastination and feel motivated to do things on a regular basis, and that's exactly what this principle helps you to do. Once you start to enjoy spending a minute on a certain thing every day you can then start increasing the amount of time you spend on the task until you realize that you want to spend more and more time doing it because it helps you get closer to your goal. This technique is a great way to teach yourself self-discipline.

Kaizen is a principle that comes from Japan and consists of two words - Kai which means 'change' and Zen which refers to wisdom. It was invented by a philosopher known as Masaaki Imai based on his own life and it has benefitted several successful business owners.

Many people surprisingly know about The Kaizen principle, but they do not pay too much attention to it because they believe that if something asks you to invest just one minute of your time it is not going to prove to be fruitful in any way. But the truth is, when you incorporate it daily and spend a minute of your routine focusing on something, it will shape your life for the better and train yourself to be more successful. There are several benefits that Kaizen has that you should make yourself aware of.

It Helps in Waste Reduction

When you implement the principles of Kaizen it helps you to save a lot of your resources that were going down the drain and enables you to identify these unnecessary expenses in your personal as well as professional life. The technique helps you identify what benefits your business and what doesn't and how you can eliminate waste and focus on the important procedures to grow your business and save resources.

Immediate Troubleshooting

When you confront a problem sooner, you manage to resolve it a lot faster. With the one-minute rule, Kaizen helps you to resolve issues almost instantly by beginning to invest just a minute a day in trying to solve it. While it may seem like a temporary solution, within a few weeks you'll realize just how far you have come and how much you managed to overcome without even realizing the amount of effort you put in.

Optimum Utilization

The amount of time required to prioritize your needs using the Kaizen process is simple and this means that it is easy to implement irrespective of how busy your life is. You don't have to worry about dealing with too many demands or limited resources anymore because Kaizen helps you to prioritize what's important and focus on eliminating anything that is necessary in your life.

Better Teamwork

When an organization implements Kaizen in the team it helps to lift spirits, and everyone starts to work using a fresh perspective that focused on a common goal which is the growth of the business rather than their own hidden agenda. When the team works together as one, it automatically reflects in the results you see in front of you and you see your business growing much faster.

Better Quality

When you start implementing Kaizen in your business, you realize that the quality of work delivered by the employees is much better and everyone starts to work in a streamlined manner. It also helps to encourage every employee to work to their full potential and this is something you will benefit from greatly.

Another great thing about the Kaizen principle is that it works in sync with everything else we have spoken about in this book so far which includes not wasting time, unnecessary brainstorming, and meetings that don't prove to be fruitful. All you need to do is ask your employees to invest a minute of their time every day and this not only encourages them to deliver four-fold results, but it makes them more positive human beings, and this will impact the entire workforce from the lowest position to top management in the organization. You will be surprised to see how one simple change can turn the business around 180 degrees.

Chapter 11:
3 Little-Known Techniques by Top Gurus

There are three key elements that you need to keep in mind in order to avoid procrastination. There are several top industry experts that have suggestions as to how you can avoid procrastination and you need to keep these tips in mind in order to be successful at what you do. Here we will look at the three tips that you probably didn't know about and these tips or techniques will help you overcome the need to procrastinate and help you take charge of your responsibilities.

Avoid Multitasking

Multitasking is a very common technique that several people use in today to cover various job responsibilities. People usually take on more than they can handle because they want to impress, and they feel that they will be able to get that much-needed promotion by working hard. When you take on too many responsibilities you will not be able to do justice to all of them and you will end up procrastinating on the less important tasks. What this eventually does this is it creates a lot of pressure on you when the smaller tasks are done. Let us take the example of an office workspace. While your prime responsibility would be to take care of your team that reports to you and ensure that performance is up to the mark, you may end up taking more responsibilities that will help you learn more at your workspace. While learning is good, taking on extra responsibilities and attending classes to improve your skills is something that will hamper your current work. When this happens, you will start feeling frustrated and you will not pay attention to what your primary responsibilities are. You will end up being so focused on what you want to do that you forget about what you must do. Procrastination is a vicious circle and once you start delaying certain responsibilities you will end up running behind when the time comes to deliver these responsibilities.

Start Enjoying Your Work

People usually avoid doing certain tasks because they don't see it as fun. A child will unlikely want to study for his math exam if he does not enjoy learning math. Similarly, you will not end up wanting to create reports in the office because you do not really enjoy doing it. While tasks like creating reports is a very monotonous job and can take a toll on you, you need to start looking at ways you can enjoy doing these tasks. When you start doing this you will avoid procrastination and it will help you complete the task. One of the best ways to avoid procrastination is when you start having fun at work. If your responsibilities at work are not fun, then you can make it fun by involving others in your duties. When you start working in collaboration you will be able to ensure that you do justice to the job and you will no longer wait till the last minute to submit a task.

Prioritize

Prioritizing is extremely important - you need to make sure that you do not undermine a task just because it is boring or difficult to complete. As we spoke about earlier, there are ways that you can delegate your responsibilities, and this is something that you should use to your advantage. When you start prioritizing and using the 10-minute rule you will be able to complete tasks more efficiently and avoid procrastination in your personal as well as your professional life.

You need to start implementing these techniques in order to become more efficient in your daily life. While procrastination maybe the easy way out, you should know that it is not a solution and you will not be able to complete anything on time if you continue hiding behind the cloak of procrastination.

Chapter 12:
How I Stopped Procrastinating (The # 1 Method)

When you achieve productivity, the first thing that someone is going to ask you is what helped you get this productive in the first place. I have written of people's productivity and how it drastically improved in a short time frame. I depended on the Pomodoro technique, which is an effective solution to help overcome procrastination and get more productive not just at your workplace but in your personal life as well. There are different things you can try and a ton of solutions you will find when it comes to overcoming procrastination. Here is what I believe, the minute you find your rhythm and you find something that works well for you, stick to it and begin improvising your behavior based on the technique that works. It is healthy to challenge yourself from time to time, but when you already have a solution that helps you better yourself and challenge yourself at your workplace and in your personal life there is no reason for you to try another technique. Using your 10-minute goal and even the 5-second rule comes in handy in certain scenarios, but if you want to plan your life and make sure that you achieve success without compromising on quality of life, then the Pomodoro technique is something I recommend you try. This is a popular concept and it has managed to stand the test of time, making it a great effective strategy to apply. The core focus of the pomodoro technique is the 80/20 rule which you need to get accustomed to. This rule pushes you to your limits and helps you train your mind to get better with each challenge that you face.

How It Works

The Pomodoro technique was invented in the 1980's for students to study more effectively without wasting time on other activities. What initially began as a training program for students turned out to be effective for people almost across the world and in different age groups. The technique is simple and is called timeboxing. We are often in situations where we can't figure out how to start a task because it seems too overwhelming. Instead of worrying about how you are going to balance out your work, most people decide to give up even before they try because they are sure they are not going to manage to get it all done. The Pomodoro technique is basically timing yourself for 25-minute intervals.

For you to use the technique you need to first identify which task you would like to begin on and how you want to work on it. Once you have a list of tasks at hand, start by prioritizing the most important ones from the less important ones and pick out the one that you must get done today.

You can decide to break down this task into several smaller portions so that it does not overwhelm you and helps you to get the job done more efficiently.

Now you need to set your pomodoro or your timer to 25 minutes. You have to continue to challenge yourself to work for an uninterrupted 25 minutes until the timer has run out. As soon as your 25 minutes is up you give yourself a quick 5-minute break. You repeat this for at least four to five times, taking quick 5-minute breaks in between, and at the end of about 5 sessions you can take a longer break which is about 20 minutes.

It's surprising how simple this technique is and yet how effectively it works not only to help you overcome your challenges but also to take on more work and deliver effective result in no time. When you know you have just 25 minutes, your brain starts to function a lot faster and you begin rationalizing the work and delegating it more effectively so that you get it done very effectively at the end of the 25 minutes. When you set a constraint, it helps you to focus more effectively because you need to get it done before the time runs out. People who lack concentration or suffer from ADD/ADHD will find this technique very helpful and they manage to get more results out of it.

When you start using the Pomodoro technique you manage to measure your results within the very first week and see if you managed to accomplish a lot more than you set out to do at the start of the week. When you limit yourself to a time constraint you start building momentum for the tasks you are working on and your productivity increases with confidence. You won't have time to second guess yourself because of the time constraint and this helps you put in effort into delivering quality work by paying more attention to what is required.

I am going to be honest with you, the Pomodoro technique may not seem like the easiest technique to adapt to when you first try it because the time constraints can be a little overwhelming. Your first few attempts may be failures and you may want to stop the timer midway so you can restart it and give yourself a little more time to work on the task at hand. After a few attempts, you will realize that it is quite efficient, and you will manage to divide your work effectively in two portions of 25 minutes so you can get the job done with ease as well as efficiency. 25 minutes may seem like a really small time window for you to complete a task but when you put your mind to it you will end up delivering a lot more than you would expect and you will realize that you can cover most of your work during the first half of the day.

It's a great hack to train your mind to focus without having to incorporate it into too many aspects in your life and this makes it simple to follow. All you need is a timer or an app to make it more interesting and you can start your journey to overcome procrastination and become more efficient.

The reason I recommend this technique is because people don't have too much time to plan daily and this is a simple rule that you won't have to remember. Once you find a technique that works for you, make sure you use it to your benefit and start converting all your procrastination habits into success stories one step at a time. You don't have to take big leaps and bounds and make huge changes in your life to achieve success and overcome procrastination. A small change can make a huge difference in your life so all you need to do is begin with that one change to start working towards a more positive and fruitful life.

Successful Tips to Help You Get Closer to Your Dream

Tips Used by A Billionaire

We all want to become successful and achieve the highest level of success in our career as well as in our personal life. While it's great for us to dream, it's important that we begin acting towards our goals if we want to turn them into a reality anytime soon. Nothing worth fighting for comes easy and you must put in a lot of effort and stay determined if you want to get closer to your goal. With a little effort and hard work, the more time you spend in self-discipline and following the right rules towards success. You will soon be able to see your goal and measure it at an arm's distance from you. It all begins with deciding to become successful and believing in yourself. You need to stop procrastinating and tell yourself that you are worth it, and you will achieve your goals no matter what. Once you have set that up, you can then follow these tips that will help you get closer to achieving your goal.

Follow Your Dreams

If you want to do something big you have to have big dreams. There's no harm in dreaming big about things you want to achieve, whether it's starting up a business or establishing something you are passionate about. The more you think about something the closer you will manage to get to it and this will help you to challenge yourself in believing that you have to work hard for it. It is important for you to visualize because when you visualize not only do you start relating to your dream, but it will help you to convert your dream into a goal that you aim at achieving.

You need to make sure that the goal or dream you set out to achieve is realistic. Once you figure out what you want to achieve then should give yourself a stipulated time frame and believe that you will achieve it by putting in a certain amount of hard work and staying determined.

Make A Positive Difference

If you want to feel good about yourself, you need to do something good from within. If you don't have a lot of money to do good you can practice humanitarian efforts by stepping outside to share a little money with a homeless man, buy him a meal, or even give him a blanket so he can stay warm. This may seem completely irrelevant to becoming successful, but the truth is when you share the little that you have with people who are less fortunate than you there is a warm feeling that takes over your heart and it makes you want to do better things for yourself. Feelings of gratitude are something that plays a huge role in becoming successful and every time you do something good you want to push yourself to work a little harder. Consider it karma - what goes around definitely comes around and when you do good to people, good eventually happens to you as well. Because people believe that doing good will eventually end up in a good result, they start putting in more effort towards the job that they have at hand and believe that the reason it is being done so effectively is because they are positive people. This is a cycle and once you understand your role in it you manage to smoothly balance out your life and continue to stay positive by contributing the little you can do to another people's life.

Believe in Your Ideas

When you dream big and you want to achieve your dreams you need to have a plan to achieve them. You will have to brainstorm vigorously in order to come up with an effective plan that won't fail you and will help you to get closer to your desired goal. Don't come up with 10 different plans and try them all to see which one works best. Put all your energy on focusing to create one foolproof idea that you know is so strong it won't fail you. Sometimes ideas do not come to you instantly and you need to take a while to think about how you can make your visions into a reality. Don't waste your time forcing yourself to come up with ideas. Do things that will calm you down and make you feel good because these are the things that can help you think more effectively. If there's too much going on in your head, clear your mind by going for walk or head to the beach and sit there for a while until you are ready. Think about the various scenarios where you could apply your business ideas and see whether it seems to be a profitable solution or not. 9 out of 10 times your solution is not going to be great, but the 10th time it will likely be the jackpot that you've always been waiting for and that's when your journey towards success truly begins. Think about innovation, think outside of the box, think about ideas no one has ever come up with. Strive to make a difference in people's life and plan effectively.

Connect with The People You Work With

When you have your own establishment or organization, focus on enjoying the kind of work you do and make sure that the people around you also enjoy themselves. Do not strive to be a boss from hell, those are the kind of people that don't get too far. Try to keep your employees as happy as possible because motivation is essential for them to be productive, and the more motivated they are the better assets they are to your organization. Look out for them and always treat them with kindness. When you provide a positive work environment for your employees they start delivering with their full potential and you will manage to get a strong group of people who strive to achieve your dream goal along with you. When you have multiple people working towards one goal the journey gets a lot shorter and it also gets easier.

Don't Give Up

Part of the journey of life is to experience failures - no matter how foolproof your methodologies are there going to be times when you face it alone. There will be problems in your life, but that doesn't mean you give up. It simply means you challenge yourself to work harder and you start stronger than you did with the previous attempt. Figure out what went wrong so you can come up with a solution to deal with the scenario in case it comes up again. You must accept failure as a part of your journey and consider it as one of the challenges that you need to deal with but always stay prepared. Businesses often encounter losses and while some of them find it difficult to deal with these losses and overcome obstacles there are others that take it with a grain of salt and move ahead. The only differences between the two organizations are planning and preparation, and determination to continue no matter what. When you start your own organization, you must keep yourself prepared for the worst and celebrate the success so that there is no loose end that could create problems for the business.

Set Yourself Up for New Challenges

A lot of business owners end up establishing their dream organization and this is where it ends - once they achieve that they no longer strive to move ahead or progress any further. This is probably the worst thing you can do because you stagnate your growth when you can truly do a lot more than you had initially set out to do. Every time you get close to achieving a goal, think about a new goal in life, so you aim at working towards it. The worst thing you can do to your brain is stop challenging it because that's when you no longer have anything to look forward to. You should live a life where you constantly look forward to doing something challenging and different and that's the reason why you must keep increasing your challenges and conquer your fears. Once you learn how to reach your first goal you should then look back at your experience and plan something on the lines of that but with a little more intensity. Within a few years you will realize that you have achieved a lot more than you initially set out to do and this will motivate you to help others do the same for themselves as well.

Spend Time with Your Family and Friends

One of the biggest challenges when you become an entrepreneur is lack of time. You may believe that you must compromise your personal life for you to achieve bigger and better things on your work front. You must remind yourself that nothing comes before your family and if you are not able to keep your family happy you will not be able to keep yourself happy. Always find time to spend with your family and never miss important occasions no matter what.

Plan your days in advance so that you never come across a situation where you need to choose between attending your child's birthday party or attending a meeting that is crucial for your business.

Hire reliable employees whom you can delegate your work to and give yourself a little room to breathe. While you should continue working on a regular basis you need to make sure that you don't bite off more than you can chew because that is where it begins to go downhill.

Get Outside

When you have a day off don't spend it in front of the television, rather, go out and enjoy nature. Plan a picnic with your family and go on spontaneous road trips just so you can have some fun away from the indoors. You need to train your children to be self-disciplined but not forget to have fun and for you to do this you got to teach them how they can enjoy life even by being successful and making the right choices. You should transform your positive energy into teaching lessons to your children from a young age because this is what helps them follow your footsteps and learn how to work hard and achieve what they want to. At the end of the day no one remembers how many hours they spent with their family in front of the television but rather the number of memories they created on trips and holidays. If you can slip in a few days of leave with your family, you can give yourself a much-needed vacation. If you want to perform as effectively and with the same zeal that you had from the day you started your journey you must keep giving yourself breaks and reminding yourself that it is fine to have fun. Don't forget how it all started and always keep your goal in mind. The trips you take and the pampering sessions you have should all be fuel for you to accomplishing small and large goals.

Prove People Wrong

There are going to be times when you come across people who might not appreciate what you do or have something bad to say to you. Don't let that affect you. One of the major reasons why people end up procrastinating is because they take to heart what another person says and forget what they can do. If someone puts you down, do not reciprocate in a negative manner but rather take it as a little criticism and work towards proving them wrong. If you believe you can truly achieve something and there are people who tell you otherwise, don't listen to them. Trust what your heart tells you and believe in the plan you set for yourself. Believing you can achieve something is one of the most effective ways to getting it done. Do not let other people tell you what you are not capable of doing. You are the best judge of that. Make sure you work hard and let people know about your success after you have achieved it. If someone tries to put you down don't tell them what you will achieve but wait for the moment to tell them what you have achieved so you can prove them wrong with confidence. Most millionaires started off broke and with no idea what they were going to do. If they decided to quit, we wouldn't have some of the biggest industries today.

Do What You Love

Just because your ideas are different from someone else's doesn't make you an odd person. It just makes you different and unique. Innovation and unique ideas are what people strive for today so when someone tells you that you are weird or unusual don't take it as criticism but consider it your uniqueness because that is what's going to help you become successful. Do crazy things in life because it will help you learn little lessons that will take you a long way. Not all your experiments are going to be successful, some may be terrible failures - but that doesn't mean you give up. It just means you must try a little harder.

Relentless and Unbeatable

No Obstacle Is Too Extreme. All It Takes Is Old School Grit and A Hardened Mind. You Can Achieve the Impossible with Mental Toughness

Introduction

Have you ever wondered what makes some people stand out and seem so unstoppable? Why do some people seem to always have things going well, and everything working in their favor?

These are not extraordinary men with special abilities. These are men that have identified limitations and everything that could be a clog in the wheel of progress. They are neither from Mars or an alternate planet. They have identified their obstacles and faced them head-on. They do not get knocked down by anything that happens to them and has developed themselves in a way that nothing can deter them.

- Have you ever wondered what these kinds of people are made of?
- What is the source of their passion and motivation?
- What keeps them going despite all odds?
- How did they get so tough that they are able to overcome the limitations of the mind?

It's no miracle, nor is there anything special that sets these people apart. These are simply people that have learned to get around the mental barrier and limitations of their mind. They possess a relentless drive to get around every obstacle set in their path. They face a task and approach it with a can-do attitude, no matter how difficult it is.

These types of people did not become like this overnight. They did not just overcome the mental barrier in a day, neither did they get their mind to stop seeing impossibilities just like that. This happened as a result of a series of effective strategies and techniques to reconfigure their mindset.

This is what this book plans to offer you. In this life-changing manual are tips, tactics, and strategies to build your mental strength. With this book, no task will ever freak you out again and the impossible will be deleted from your dictionary.

To everyone out there ready to bring out the best in themselves and set daring goals and face them head-on, you will find this book very helpful.

With cognitive behavioral therapy, you can completely alter your mindset and become a fearless person who sees possibility in everything.

Chapter 1:
An Unbeatable Mind

Many times, humans are faced with certain problems that may seem insurmountable and the nature of man, which seems to possess many weaknesses, will not always serve as a guide if he does not rely on the strengths that are within him. Therefore, relying solely on these weaknesses only places one on the path to failure. Although a person might have set out to achieve success at all cost, situations or conditions may not favor the goals that they have set out to achieve. These conditions come in different shapes and forms of barriers and stumbling blocks. However, one cannot just pretend that these barriers are not real. The truth is, they are as real as they come and if not faced with caution, can bring a whole year or even a decade's effort to futility. In all cases, the first thing to note is the fact that these barriers are only physical, and it only goes to explain why they are so prominent. However, inside of you is a strong weapon that can break every barrier and chain - your mind.

To begin, let's try to pin a definition or maybe a face, to the mind. It is often described by experts as the core of everyone's existence. The mind is the seat of every human's wisdom as well as the center of one's consciousness. A person without a mind may as well be considered non-existent. According to scientists, the mind is the product of activities of the brain. While the brain is the physical property, the mind is the product of those active senses. However, recent research has proved that the mind isn't merely the physical activities of the brain; it goes way beyond that. Although the brain plays a very important role in the workings of the mind, it can't be confined to a compartment of the skull or even the entire body. According to extensive research by scientists, the mind is not just our perception of experiences, but the experiences itself. It is said that one cannot separate the subjective view of humans' perception of the world from his interaction with the world. Therefore, this brings us to the point where the mind is meant to control the activities of a man with his world, no matter the possibilities and impossibilities, constraints, and barriers. Certainly, the demands of everyday living may be so tasking that sometimes, they may seem impossible to surmount. In hard times, the only way to get above these situations is to put one's mind to work. You may wonder how that is possible if the mind is already preoccupied, if not weighed down with thoughts of what could have been and what isn't. The first step to breaking through, however, is to realize that these things only exist in your brain and in the physical. Once you realize this, you will find out that there is an endless scope of what you can achieve in your mind. You may want to imagine why people tend to give up on things easily when they feel like they have easier options, like, 'how do you expect me to stay up for three hours studying, when I can split my study hours between different days, especially when I do not have a deadline to meet?' Sometimes, it feels impossible to stay awake once you pick a book or sit down to write a term paper. When deadlines begin to stare us in the face, these impossibilities disappear completely. Suddenly, someone that could not initially focus for three hours can now go for five hours without even blinking. The fear of dropping from an 'A' to 'F' suddenly keeps you on your toes and makes you go to lengths that you previously considered impossible. This goes to show that sleepiness, time, and everything that served as a limitation was merely a product of the physical world, and they have nothing on your mind.

Once you set your mind to it, you can achieve it. The following are ways the mind can turn limitations to possibilities.

Limitations Can Bring Out Your Creative Side

Do you remember the saying; necessity is the father of invention? Here's how it works: once you are faced with a tedious task that seems impossible, there may be only two ways out; to quit or to keep moving. If you quit, it was never so important to you, so you keep moving even though it seems impossible and to an outsider, you look like another joker on the path to failure. At this point, if you have chosen success, your mind automatically sets itself to look for ways to succeed. It is like you have been pushed to the wall and you now must fight back to liberate yourself. Such is the story of a certain young screenwriter, whose reputation seems to be on the line, as he is faced with the challenge of providing his viewers with equally interesting new episodes to his soap opera, which has since become an all-time favorite. Having added very interesting twists to his story, the life of his main character, who is the kernel of the show, is cut short as he dies in a fatal car crash. The writer now must decide if the show will die with the main character or not. In the mind of others, this might seem like a great limitation to the show, but it is at this point that the creativity of the writer will have to come into play. Ordinarily, this may be a dead end, but the limitation posed by the death of one character may be a push for a new/fresh start if the writer puts his creative mind to work. The possibilities are endless; all he needs is to tap into them. The physical limitations you see might just be the push you need to be more creative. Instead of listening to the voices in your head, it is always better to trust your mind and explore all the chances it creates.

The Central Governor Theory Versus the Placebo Effect

There is a theory that states that a part of a human's brain controls the energy supply and shuts the body down as a protective measure so that no permanent harm will come to it. This part of the body is called the central government and this theory claims that this governor has a conservative nature, so it sends pain signals to the body, making it seem as though it cannot take more pain way earlier than the body needs it. This is as a form of protection for the body to get some rest before the supply of energy is completely exhausted. Once this central governor sends its signal, one is meant to think that he cannot go further and is therefore compelled to shut down and take some rest. The catch here is that the point when you are given this signal isn't the point when you are exhausted. Therefore, it takes determination to beat this signal and go further. This is only made possible by the mind.

Let's take the example of a kid that was made to run a marathon with much bigger kids at his school's sports competition. Once the race started, he seemed to be lagging and he soon began to feel exhausted. Not even the loud cheers from the crowd could propel him to go further. This is because the central government has already told him that he cannot go further and the gap between him and his bigger competitors doesn't seem to be helping either. Obviously, he isn't going to make it anywhere close to the top, so he would rather just quit. From the sideline, however, he is handed an energy drink and he gulp it with enthusiasm. Hopefully, the drink will be able to boost his strength. Surprisingly, he begins to get more energy and like magic, he starts closing in on the wide gap between himself and the closest person to him. He starts to pass more people than he could ever have imagined and as it was down to the last lap, it became obvious that he was going to finish well. He ended up finishing amongst the top three and that was a great achievement for him as he didn't appear to be as big as the rest of the kids in the race. If he was to thank anyone, it would have to be the person that handed him the drink from the sideline and maybe even the company that produced the drink.

What he didn't know was that it was all his mind at work. Once the central governor presented him with the red signals because he wasn't doing well, his mind began to lose faith in his abilities. The drink, however, didn't quite have an energy boosting component. It was just a placebo drink and once he gulped it, the placebo effect made him start trusting in the strength of the drink, therefore boosting his confidence. This goes to prove that most times, when your body starts telling you to stop, it is the brain that is safeguarding itself and, you have so much more to give. Although this theory is yet to be fully confirmed by scientists, it has been proven that something happens in the brain once you begin to expand an ample amount of energy. The drink, believed to be an energy booster, sent a signal to the brain, telling it that help has come. Thanks to this, it picks itself up, making you feel like your lost energy has been replenished. This means that most of the time, when your brain tells you that you can no longer go further because you are tired, you aren’t tired. It is the almighty governor doing its job and with enough mindfulness, you can overcome this.

When you begin to gain control over your mind and thoughts, you begin to incredibly push the limits and do greater things than you could have ever imagined. In this case, your mind helps you realize what is really happening when your brain tells you that you can no longer go further. You will now realize that it is your brain that is craving some rest, but it doesn’t mean you have reached your limit. Over time, you will be able to build your mental resilience when you understand the urge to quit and recognize it for what it is.

Don't Avoid Struggles, Seek Them Out

Most times, people tend to run away from struggles because they think that they are not strong enough to handle them. As you may already know, you are stronger than you think and if you are mindful enough, you can achieve much more than you have ever imagined. Aside from that fact that struggles help you gather experiences and knowledge, they also help you become stronger. Also, struggles help you become a better person and build your mental ability, so instead of trying to avoid them by laying on the couch watching TV, why not tap into the benefits that these struggles present and make the best out of them by facing them head-on. This will help you build your mental resilience. To do this, try to constantly push harder by testing your limits. Each time you do this, you will get a bit better. Of course, things will not get easier; they are bound to get more difficult as you proceed, but as you surmount each phase, you will grow and gather more mental and physical capacities to handle more difficulties. Let's say you are doing a squats routine. If you did fifty squats yesterday, today is the time to do ten more. Chances are that the previous day, once you reached forty squats, you thought you would collapse if you did even one more, but just a day later, you went all the way to fifty and are still standing. Today, forty will not feel that difficult anymore and later, you will go above fifty as you gradually get used to it.

When you become mindful, you realize that the thing you had so much fear for isn't that difficult after all. Soon, it becomes such a habit that you take up other challenges to keep you on your toes. It's all in your mind, so instead of seeking comfort, you can set out to push your limits.

When you set your mind to be tough and rugged, you will discover that there is almost nothing you can't do. Maybe the Biblical story of David and Goliath wasn't about divine power at work. It could have just been about a little man doing his absolute best because he knew everything in his existence depended on it. His brain may have seen a Goliath, but his mind saw a defeat able person, and indeed, he was able to triumph.

No matter what the physical tells you, all you need is to trust in the power of your mind. If your mind is set on achieving success, you will surely excel.

Chapter 2:
The Right Attitude Is A Must

In life, you come across different people, go to different places, and experience different emotions. All these are what form your life experience. Now, have you ever wondered why two people may experience the same scenario differently? It is all about the state of your mind, which is simply your mindset. What may be difficult or scary to you may be fun and easy to someone else. The difference between you and the other person isn't farfetched. While you see a task as a challenge, the other person may see it as an adventure, and this is the reason why it will be a difficult task for you and not for the other person.

According to Charles R. Swindoll, life is 10% what happens to you and 90% how you perceive it. When faced with a challenge, however, it is up to you to choose whether to be reactive or proactive. When you allow your emotions to get the best of you and react according to the adrenaline rush in case of an emergency, chances are you will become overwhelmed by situations and lose control of everything. This means that when such things happen, you won't be able to handle them the way you should. It is a fact that there are times when emotions become so overwhelming that it may become impossible to not react to them, and when this happens, you must put your mind to work. If you become drawn to those emotions, it may be hard to get control of the situation. It may not even be something tied to emotion that seems to be overwhelming you, as it could be a certain procedure, an addiction, or just a phase. It is normal to get trapped in such situations. What makes you a strong person, however, is your ability to set your mind on your goal and evaluate the right and the not-so-right. In such situations, you have two choices; you can either be proactive or reactive.

If you are reactive, you will be highly affected by your environment. When things are good, you feel good, and when they aren't you feel terrible and almost always allow the tide of things to affect the way you perform and react. However, if you are proactive, you can set back and evaluate situations regardless of what effect they may have on you. The moment you feel down or when you seem to have been hit by a very hard blow, you have the power to catapult yourself to the point of absolute empowerment and strength.

In everything, consider being proactive, because in life, we are more inclined to choose the easy path as opposed to the difficult yet more profitable one. This may be a very difficult decision, but to become a proactive person, there are always steps to take. First, you must take responsibility for everything that happens, because this is what distinguishes you from a reactive person. As a proactive person, you oversee your life and don't let external situations influence it. To do this, you must focus on things that are within your control. You see, there are some things that are absolutely beyond our control; such things will be the way they are no matter how much we brood over them. Instead of focusing your energy on such things, it is always better to look at the bright side and use the little or maybe not so little ray of light to your own advantage. Often, we can control the efforts, time and investment we put into certain things, but the results may not be entirely under our control. Therefore, when it comes to results, we must lay back to see what they turn out to be. This can be extremely difficult for some people, but the more we invest our time in things that we cannot control, the more time we lose neglecting the things that we can control, which may turn out to our advantage. Also, the problems may seem like much more than we can handle and the thought of them can be totally overwhelming. Instead of focusing on these problems, why not focus on the solutions? When you think about your problems too much, you create more problems by disarming yourself. Instead, you can gather strength by focusing your mind on the solutions. As soon as problems surface, think of how to solve them. In a way, these problems are part of the things you cannot control because they are already there. The part which you can control, however, is the possible way(s) to get rid of the problems. As a proactive person, you are already used to solving problems, so it's not a difficult thing to do at any point. You have discovered that the fastest way to get ahead in life is to act by finding a solution to your problem. Remember, when you focus on your problems, this creates more problems.

Consistency is another key aspect of being productive. If, at any point, you find that you are becoming indecisive, understand that you have derailed from the path of proactivity. As a proactive person, you must lean towards habits that propel you to achieving your goals. When you are consistent, you make progress, even if it feels like you are taking tiny inconsequential steps. With time, those seemingly small steps will earn you great results.

Your Life Depends on Your Mindset

In life, you have the power to change the way you see things, your perception of the people you come across, as well as your experiences. What you make of everything is largely up to you. Therefore, it is believed that you oversee your life. As discussed earlier, you can be a reactive person and leave your life to fate by letting everything slide, or you can be a proactive person and take absolute control of it. All this is a product of your mind and to excel, you need a positive mindset towards life.

The good thing is that we are in control of one of the most important tools in our existence, our mind. As each day passes by, we have the chance to make each minute meaningful by changing things to work in our favor. Sad day? Make yourself happy by looking at the good side of the bad experience. There is often so much to gain from one single thought, so take a deep breath and listen to your mind. A life-changing idea may just be about to pop in.

As a kid, there was a fairytale about a farmer who lived in a farmhouse that taught me how to see the good side of situations. One day, his only horse left home and did not return at night. His neighbors gathered to share their sympathy, and in such an unfortunate situation, they said, "how can this happen to you?" This farmer, almost unbroken, had only one thing to say: "Life goes on". The day after, his horse returned with a wild horse and having gone out to see if the new horse belonged to anyone, he discovered that he might just have to expand his barn to accommodate two horses. His good neighbors all gathered again, but this time to jubilate with him. Again, the farmer said, "Life goes on". The third day, the farmer's son went out with the wild horse, and while riding, he had an accident and broke his leg, and of course, the neighbors gathered and again, the farmer said, "Life goes on". A day after, Nazi soldiers went from house to house to recruit young men to join the army. When they got to the farmer's house, they rejected his son because he had a bad leg. Therefore, thanks to this farmer, I learned not to dwell on my problems. Though this is just a fairytale, the farmer did not dwell on his problems too much, even though it seemed like there was a new one every day. This is how we should lead our lives; instead of going on and on about the things that have gone wrong, the farmer chose to focus on the future. Unlike the farmer though, we are advised to find permanent solutions while keeping our eyes on the future.

Although you must look at the bright side, it is important to be realistic. Remember that your life is not a fairytale, so you must take absolute charge of it. Try to be as forgiving as possible, and make sure you take a lesson from everything and everyone you come across. Somewhere, somehow, something great lurks around the corner, waiting to be found. Make sure you are determined to find it. Knowledge is power, so make sure your arm yourself with it by constantly searching for it. The fact that you do not know something does not mean that it does not exist. It also does not mean that it exists either, but if you don't attempt to find it, you will continue to live in oblivion, so step out of your comfort zone to enrich your mind. This single piece of information may be what you need to make a life-changing decision.

There are mistakes that are okay to make, as you can always learn from them. However, it is terrible to beat yourself up about them. Remember, they are in the past, and your past is one of the things you cannot change, so never focus on your mistakes and rather move ahead and implement the lessons you have learned from them. Do not think anyone is looking at the things you have done wrong, because in reality no one really cares, and you are the only one focusing so much on those mistakes. Life goes on, so move along with it so that you are not left behind because things are going to keep happening, with or without you.

Taking a moment to look within yourself works like magic. Pause and reevaluate your existence. Just sit with yourself and exist. Remind yourself of the things you stand for and the things that make you who you are. Look at the things you want from life, create dreams, and chase them. There are things that will exist between you and those dreams, and it is now up to you to either consider them obstacles that can hold you back, or forms of encouragement that will propel you to achieve greater things. Everything borders on your mindset and the way you interpret obstacles has to do with your perception and interpretation, which are core components of your existence. Remember we talked about consistency? Now, try to look at the mirror and look at yourself from someone else's point of view. Can you recognize the person in the mirror? If the answer is yes, it means that you have been consistent enough. If you said no, it means that somewhere along the line, you have deviated from the person you used to be. Maybe you need to retrace your steps, or perhaps change is what you need to get to the place you need to be. You don't have to be rigid; change when you should but do not be unnecessarily wavered. If you find out that you are beginning to lose control, maybe it is time to get your life back and take charge of it. Always remember that what lays in your mind has the full power to make or spoil your life. It all depends on you.

Chapter 3:
A Navy SEAL'S Mindset

Navy SEALs are known to be the most well-trained special force in the US Military and are even regarded by some as the most well-trained special force in the world. From BUDS training, Hell Week, and every other activity in the quest to become a Navy SEAL, it is not a weak mind's job to successfully complete the Navy SEAL training. Many people believe that being a Navy SEAL has everything to do with a person's physical structure, but this is not true because most times, the physique of a person doesn't go a long way to determine the success of a person in Navy SEAL training. You are probably wondering what determines the success of a Navy SEAL. Is it luck, genetics or fate, one may ask? Well, the reality is that the success of the Navy SEAL is not determined by the body, but by the mind.

According to experts, the SEAL training is specially designed to push you to the edge repeatedly until you either break or become tough and able to take up any task with confidence.

Don't Procrastinate

Procrastination is a killer of dreams. Whenever you think of an idea and you do not act when you are supposed to, those dreams are as good as dead. Procrastination makes you think you still have time, but the truth is, if you are not using it properly, time will never be enough. There is absolutely no difference between you and the multimillionaire that keeps cashing out despite bad government policies and even sometimes recession. You and the man that never cries about hard times have the strongest tool to succeed ever - time. Every single person has the same 24 hours to make a difference. Once you step out of your bed, make sure you achieve the things that you have thought of in your mind. The conditions may not be right, such as facing bad weather, or if your car has just broken down, but those are only physical limitations, and you have the power to rise above the odds. Never say tomorrow as tomorrow never ends. Take that step today because now is the perfect time. It is important to do what is right, but it is even more important to do what is right when it's right. When you push activities aside, you may be setting yourself up for undue pressure. When you eventually decide to do the things that you have postponed for so long, you may be faced with limited time or worse still, you may not be able to meet the deadlines at all because so much time has passed with you telling yourself that you will do what you were supposed to do some other time. It may be the pressure of having to deal with so many activities that is weighing you down. Think of the SEAL whose life in BUDS training is always all about overcoming different trials yet must set goals for himself in order to get to the finish line. Procrastination is never a thing for a Navy SEAL; in fact, a SEAL is incomplete without challenges and what makes him successful is his ability to attack those challenges head-on. No matter how difficult it may seem, a Navy SEAL is trained to overcome difficult/life-threatening challenges. This should be the mindset of anyone that wants to get anywhere close to success. Attack any task as it comes, and never leave it to later, because if you can do it later, you can do it now as well. Always keep a notepad at hand, and whenever you think that you may have thought of a brilliant idea, jot it down. This is because spontaneous ideas can slip through your fingers with the speed of a jellyfish so do not wait; write it down and act on it as fast as possible.

Discipline Is Not Punishment, Embrace Your New Habits

There are times when you must face consequences for your reaction to things you have done or have failed to do. Other times, you just must step out of your comfort zone to put yourself in a better place to achieve the things you want. Whenever you are faced with such scenarios, keep in mind that you are going through a disciplinary phase and can only get better at it. A Navy SEAL goes through more than a thousand experiences where they must sacrifice their comfort for a greater goal. During Hell Week, a BUDS candidate is said to be allowed only four hours of sleep during the whole week. Worse still, during the training, their resilience is tested on so many fronts, which is why the Navy SEAL isn't about physical fitness, but more about mental fitness. Sometimes, when a BUDS candidate is underwater with SCUBA gear, an instructor creeps in to yank the oxygen mask off from him. That's not all; the instructor then ties the candidate's oxygen line in a knot. A feeble-minded candidate will only see this as a punishment and even a death sentence, so instead of letting himself die, he would rather give up and leave the training camp. Others who are successful at the training will see this as just another challenge and will find a way to get their gear to work again in order to breathe. This will happen repeatedly. However, the product of this exercise is to help the candidate attain the highest possible level of discipline, amongst other things. In the future, while facing life-threatening situations, instead of panicking, the candidate will look for the root cause of the situation to get themselves back in shape. In the face of such difficulty, instead of seeing it as an attack on your person, or as a punishment for your past failures, the SEAL learns that it is just another phase of their training and they only have one choice, which is to succeed. Those who will become successful will not see a disciplinary action as a punishment, but as sacrifices needed to be made to become better.

When you lose sleep over a project you are currently undertaking, you must see it as a necessity and a step to make you stronger and better. Do not beat yourself up for taking up such a humongous task that is taking so much from you. Always keep in mind that you are stronger than the task. As stated in the earlier sections of this book, there is a lesson to learn from every single experience or person you meet. In the same light, pay keen attention to the details and the tiny bits of lessons you learn from any disciplinary phase you encounter. In the future, this will help you tackle similar situations. These lessons may be immaterial, but they will certainly come in handy. Just like a Navy SEAL whose scuba gear has been yanked off, instead of simply relying on your impulse, you have made it a habit to calm your nerves. Make sure you carry this habit with you and apply it in other scenarios when your nerves seem to be raging.

The 10-Second Rule

Sometimes, things get so intense that the only thing you can be at that moment is confused. At such times, if someone asks you to describe your state of mind, you may only have one word; confused. Well, this is normal; even the best sometimes gets confused too, but it shouldn't last for too long. When one gets to that point, several impulses begin to pop up and you may even be tempted to act on these impulses. Well, taking impulsive decisions is as dangerous as not making a move at all. If you make a wrong move based on your impulse, everything you have built over time can come crashing down. Psychologists say most impulsive decisions are most likely irrational. Let's say you are driving by the corner and a cyclist has just crashed into you. Your impulse will automatically give you signals to rush out of the car and rage at the fact that the cyclist may have just destroyed your bumper. If you act on that impulse, there is a possibility to lose more than just your bumper: perhaps your phone was on your lap at the time of the crash and as you were rushing out, you dropped it and stepped on it, therefore causing more damage by crushing your phone's screen. In these types of situations, the 10-second rule comes in handy. So, in this scenario, once you notice that you have been crashed into, the best thing to do is to take a few seconds (ten seconds is recommended) to take a deep breath and recollect yourself. Within these seconds, you have the chance to recollect yourself and make a more rational decision. Now, you will have the chance to pull yourself together and save yourself the agony of losing even more due to the incident.

Let's revisit the SEAL whose SCUBA gear has been yanked off; if when he notices that his gear is off, he acts on impulse, he might panic, and this may lead to him drowning. SEALS, however, are experts in calming their nerves, so they will not be so impulsive. They therefore typically apply the 10-second rule, so they take ten seconds to recollect themselves before making any move. This helps to save a lot of things and in the end, you will be grateful for those short ten seconds you have taken. On its own, ten seconds may be a bit inconsequential, but its value is priceless, so the next time you are on the edge, instead of trusting your impulse which isn't reliable, take a moment to apply the 10-second rule.

Do Things Others Won't do

Most times, going with the crowd makes you fit in, but you do not want to just be another person in the crowd, as it is better to stand out than to fit in. Being the only one doing things differently may seem weird but in the end, it will certainly pay off. Here's the catch: when you must do the same thing as many other people, think of a unique way to go about it. It doesn't mean you are doing it wrong; there are a thousand and one ways to do things, so don't stick to the common one. These common ways may be stereotypical. It is left for you to find the other narrative and stick to it, and in the end, you will be a bit above the rest.

This will be a bit daring but it will help a lot. When every other person seems to be going the same way, this must mean that it's the easy way, and it may possibly lead to getting 60 percent of the desired result, which is just a little bit above average. Well, it's a passing mark, right? You are way better than that and if you set your mind towards it, you can do much better. Try doing it differently; don't go in the same direction as 99 percent of the others. Look at the other possible but not so easy options and choose the one that best suits your purpose. If you find the drive and pursue it, you will be able to achieve more than the others.

Think Long Term

There is a goal for every activity that you indulge in. Sometimes, the immediate goal may not really be worth it. Well, you need to remember that what you are doing is not for immediate gains. Think beyond tomorrow and think long-term.

The Navy SEALs are said to always be setting goals for themselves. When facing a hard time, like the SEAL, think of the things you wish to achieve in the future. Before enrolling for a special force in the US Army, passion is an important driving force so when they go through all the rigorous tasks, they keep setting their sights on the bigger picture, which is the main reason why they enrolled in the first place. When they are underwater, they keep telling themselves that they cannot quit, because, first, they do not want to die, and second, they remind themselves that while quitting will give them temporary relief, they will later regret the fact that they didn't carry on because quitting means giving up on their dreams.

The 3-3-3 rule is very potent in this aspect. When you are taking a decision, think about the effect it will have in the next three months. Let's say you didn't plan for a child but just discovered that you are pregnant; you now have two choices, to get rid of the pregnancy or to have the baby. Before you decide what to do, think of the effect it will have on you in the nearest and distant future. Are you going to abort the baby? Well, this may give you the chance to pursue everything you wish to achieve and may make you feel good for a short while, but what happens in the next three years? If you are going to decide to start having babies then, what happens if you are unable to conceive? Then, in the next three decades, if you are still not able to conceive, how will you feel? Maybe things will not turn out this way, and you may be able to conceive at the time you plan to in the future, and the only thing you will have to deal with is your conscience. If this doesn't really feel like a consequence you are willing to face in the future, maybe you should try the next option, especially when it's not like you never wanted to have babies at all. Now, the other option is to keep the baby, right? Think of the phases of pregnancy; in three months, you will be in your first trimester, which is the most difficult phase of your pregnancy journey. How are you going to deal with the morning sicknesses, the hormonal imbalance, and so many other changes in your metabolism? In three years, remember that you must deal with some physical changes. You will now have to be responsible for someone else - are you going to live up to the task? What about the next three decades? What or who will that child be? At that time, will all the trouble be worth it? Does it look like a long-term goal you are willing to achieve? Now, weigh your options and choose the one that is best for you.

Life Isn't A Competition

When you are striving to be a better person than you were yesterday, focus on yourself because you are all that matters. Do not wage yourself against somebody else because you want to compete with them, as they are also running their own race, and everyone will get to where they are meant to be time. When you focus too much on someone else, you lose focus on your own self and this doesn't help your journey in any way.

In anything that you do, strive to be better by constantly improving with all the resources and time at your disposal. Being better than the person you were yesterday is a goal that you must achieve. In fact, the only person you should want to be better than is your old self. Keep improving by the day; no amount of improvement can be enough, but don't ever think of wanting to be better than someone else. Of course, it is good to be better than someone else, but don't make it a goal. Being better than someone else comes naturally, so don't force it. Keep working hard to improve, don't stop, and remember - the sky is wide enough for every bird to fly.

Chapter 4:
Simple Yet Effective Strategies to Strengthen the Mind

The mind is the kernel of everything that has to do with every individual, from a single idea to the huge milestones accomplished. It all starts from the mind and the healthier your mind is, the faster it becomes, and it becomes capable of things that would ordinarily seem impossible. Therefore, people are often advised to take their mental health seriously. It is never a good thing to have a mind that is void of ideas, so when people perform below expectations, we hear stuff like: "you must be out of your mind". In order not to be out of one's mind, one needs to strive to always feed the mind to become healthier and stronger. Daily activities can alter your state of the mind, especially when you live in a city that seems to have so many crazy things. In such cases, a person is faced with the battle of trying to keep a sane mind. On your own, this may be very difficult as so many factors contribute to keeping your mind healthy. Therefore, one must make conscious efforts to keep their mind healthy. The following are some tips to do so:

Wake up early and get out of bed: Sleep is a good thing and it would be detrimental to your health to not get enough of it. Just like everything that has a good side, it is wrong to spend most of your time sleeping. This will not only make you come across as a lazy person, but it also puts your mind in a state of idleness. Nothing productive ever comes out of an idle mind. Everyone is advised to get at least six hours of sleep. This means that if you go to bed by 10 PM, you shouldn't be up before 4 AM.

However, there is a huge difference between waking up and getting out of bed. Some people can take up to three hours to get up from their bed after waking up. While this habit gives one time to accommodate as many thoughts as possible, it also gives him time to leave so many things undone. So, this means that after getting enough sleep, a person is expected to wake up and get out of bed early. It is a known fact that every fresh morning offers enough energy to do much more than you will in the afternoon or at night, except in case of sickness. Once your mind, body, and brain have rested enough at night, your mind is re-energized, and you can do much more in the morning. The thing is that during your daily activities, you have very little control over how the day will turn out. That's why it's important for you to get up early to program your mind to work the way you want it to be so that you can set the tone for the rest of the day.

Make your bed: Once you get out of bed, don't just walk away. Take a few seconds to look back at the mess you made while sleeping. Do you want to leave that mess behind? I guess you wouldn't like to start your day on that note, so take some time to make your bad. This has both a physical and mental effect on you. The time you use to make your bed gives you the chance to think. You will be able to think of the things you want to achieve that day. Also, you will be able to articulate yourself and get yourself together before even stepping in the shower. On the other hand, this simple exercise will boost your mental strength. Looking at your neatly made bed will automatically make you feel tidy and this is necessary to set the tone for the day. As you have already started the day on that note, you will possibly want every part of your day to be like that, starting from the remaining parts of your room. Oh! That shirt isn't in its right place, so put it where it needs to be, and the same goes for every other thing and like magic, you will find out that you ran through the remaining part of your day calm and collected.

Carry heavy shit: Your physical and mental wellbeing works together, and therefore it is important to be as physically as mentally fit. Every day make sure you test your strength by trying to lift something heavy. This will help you flex your muscles as well as remind you that you have so much energy lurking within you. You may not have the time to go to the gym or the willpower to take on an exercise routine. Lifting something heavy once or twice will help you make up for the little exercise you are missing out on.

Study first: There is nothing more important than reading books. Every book has a unique idea to offer, so always make sure you pick up a book and look out for that singular idea that will work for you, no matter how little it may seem. Reading can create new ideas within you and light up your imagination. This is because the ideas imbibed in a book do not exist in isolation. As you are digesting it, it interacts with some of the knowledge that you already have and the idea you can gain from each book, no matter how small, will add more flavor to the state of your mind.

Eat something you don't like: The importance of eating healthy can never be overemphasized. Food is an integral requirement of your everyday life. So, it is important to eat good food, even if you do not like its taste. For example, kids are known to hate vegetables even though they are very good for their health. The fact that they do not like them doesn't mean that parents won't give it to them. Typically, parents and food companies find ways of infusing it into children's diets without them realizing it. You can employ the same strategy. Maybe you hate carrots, but you need Vitamin A for better sight; so, instead of avoiding it, you can simply blend it into your food and make it a way of adding color to it. This goes for every other food you do not like. Remember that a healthy diet is the cradle of good health, so make sure you eat well. You do not have to like the food; just eat what is right because it is important for your health.

Chapter 5:
From Fragile to a Champions Mind

In this chapter, I am going to show you how to transform your mind from the unconscious programming that has led you to believe that you have been stripped of your innate ability to be a winner. If you follow the strategies outlined here (and in other chapters of this book), you will feel like screaming from the rooftop "bring it on, world, bring it on!"

You Are Your Own Leader

From birth and all through your childhood, you have been accustomed to look up to others (parents, guardians, influential persons) for direction and leadership. They told you what to do, how to do it, and when to do it, and you accepted it all; line, hook, and sinker. Well, that was in your formative years. As an adolescent, your instinct to rebel against ideas that do not resonate with you began to surface, but if you are like most people, those instincts were quickly squelched by the people you looked up to. They prefer to keep you under control; that way, they can lead you to the "right path."

Docile and broken, a lot of people allowed that type of programming to govern their lives even into adulthood, and it reflects in every facet of their lives. They look up to governments to make their economy better, look up to their bosses to make their working conditions better or to give them directions, and look up to their partners (spouses, business associates, etc.) to tell them if what they are doing is in order or not. At best, most people only offer suggestions and hope that those suggestions have a favorable response.

Athletes are not immune to this type of programming or upbringing, so it is not surprising to find athletes with very strong minds. Just observe an athlete (or any individual for that matter) and see how they make up their minds about a course of action, and you can tell if they are operating from a fragile or an unbeatable mindset. But the good news is, even if you are operating from the subconscious programming of a fragile mind, you can turn that around. And here's exactly how to do that.

- Recognize that you are an individual with a complete mind of your own.
- Accept that you have the sole responsibility for the outcomes of your decision.
- Challenge your mind to come up with decisions and answers without waiting for someone else.
- Pay attention to suggestions from external sources but allow your mind to decide if those suggestions are fit for you or not.
- Do not be afraid to make decisions.
- Do not be afraid to make the wrong decisions.
- Give yourself permission to voice your views.

I am not in any way suggesting disregarding constituted authority. I am only stating the obvious: you do not have to rely on anyone to know what to do and how to do it. The truth is, every possible method that has been proposed to perform an action was from someone's mind – a mind that took charge and was not afraid to be put to test. Such minds are in no way better than yours! You are well-equipped and capable of looking inwards to determine what suits you best and to come up with decisions based on your deep convictions. If you really want to succeed and stand out from the crowd, don't wait for directions. You must carve out a path and tread it without caring if anyone is following or not. Remember, others have the inalienable right to direct their own lives too.

It takes practice, but when you begin to give your mind the permission to come up with its own ideas, it is like exercising a muscle; with time, it will develop, and soon, you can make split-second decisions that are very sound and have positive outcomes.

You are the boss of your life. Always remember that! It is time to take back the wheels of control and flush out the feebleness and flawed programming drummed into you during your formative years. Authority figures are good, but you must understand that you are an authority of your own!

There's Always Room for Improvement

What's your highest achievement? Really, what is it? Write it down. Now, below that, write in bold letters, "I CAN DO BETTER THAN THIS!" (And make sure to include the exclamation mark). Please, when doing this exercise, do not type the words using your computer, phone, tablet, or any other device. Use a pen and paper, as there is a flow of energy that occurs when you write words with your hands from your mind onto a paper. It is like birthing an idea from the realm of the unseen (the mind) into physical reality (paper). That is the very first step to creating from your mind.

You see, no matter your level of achievement, your mind can think of several other ways to do better than your previous achievement. Remember Napoleon Hill's famous quote? "*Whatever the mind of man can conceive and believe, it can achieve.*" Now, that's not just some fine saying; it is a fact. There is no limit whatsoever that exists in your mind except what you have accepted as your limits. We have spoken about this in Chapter 1, as we mentioned that there are physical limits but none whatsoever for the mind (kindly go back to Chapter 1 if you skipped it).

I'll let you in on a little secret that can change your entire life and career. Most of us are guilty of settling for a standard we accept instead of striving for the success we have imagined for ourselves. You can surpass whatever you have accomplished in the past unless you have decided to settle for your past achievement as your peak accomplishment. In that case, you have accepted a standard instead of continuing to strive to greater heights.

Realize that once you have accomplished a task or reached a milestone in your life or your career, that accomplishment is in the past. Basking in it is simply living in the past! While there is nothing wrong with enjoying the good feeling that comes with reaching your goals, dwelling on it is the same as telling your mind that you have reached your destination, so it can take a break and circle back to that point whenever the need arises. This makes it impossible for you to go beyond that success level. Do you see how a feeble mind can keep you stuck perpetually? And if you find yourself in a situation where you seem not to be able to surpass your previous achievements, it is time to break free from the vicious circle. Here's how.

- Do the exercise above, i.e., write down your highest achievement and in bold letters write "I CAN DO BETTER THAN THIS!"

- In your mind's eye, visualize yourself breaking your own records, no matter how laudable they are.

- Challenge your mind to think of ways to improve on your previous accomplishments.

Remember your past actions that brought about those accomplishments and begin to take greater and more intelligent actions that are sure to produce greater results (read the section *Start Counting When You're Tired*).

More Than One Way

There is no beeline to success, so quit looking for it. You will make mistakes! That's a given. When you understand and accept this fact, you will save yourself the heartache of wallowing in self-pity because your attempt at success didn't yield the result you wanted. However, if you acknowledge that mistakes or temporal setbacks are what make you do something better the next time, there is no room to categorize your mistakes as a failure. When others see that you have failed, this creates a clear pathway to improving by doing the same thing in a better way.

A feeble mind easily accepts failure. An unbeatable mind does not recognize the word "failure" – it simply forges ahead despite failure. Come to think of it - why should you accept failure when there is obviously more than one way to do something? Do you see why it is important to give your mind permission to think for itself? If you do, your mind is intelligent enough to come up with dozens of ways for you to do one thing. So, if one way does not yield the expected result, don't just shut down your mind, throw your hands in the air in exasperation and cry "I know I'm not cut out for this stuff!" Yes, you are, but only if you will allow your mind to show you other ways to do the same thing.

Look intelligently at your past failures and you will see that because you improved on them, you were able to succeed at things that seemed impossible before. I love using the example of the latest automobiles. For example, look at the design of the 1964 Mercedes Benz 220 series. Considering that in retrospect, it is a complete failure compared to the performance of the latest series. However, designers and engineers kept on improving on past failures until the present 2019 Mercedes Benz CLS series. And if you think that is an awesome model, wait until 2050 and you may consider the latest model a complete failure too.

But I am not just referring to cars. I am asking you to look at your very first achievement in your field and see how far you've come. If you've been in your field for around 5 years, you will notice that your early achievements would be considered gross underperformance if you were to repeat those "feats" now. In other words, your mind constantly strives to outperform its previous achievements, but only if you allow it.

So, stop seeing failure as the end of the road. It is only a pathway to create numerous other paths for you to explore. If you approach your endeavors with this mindset, nothing can stop you from attaining your goals.

Pressure Brings Out the Best in You

10 months ago, your maximum pushup count was 100. Today, it is still 100. Does that not tell you there is something fundamentally wrong with your mind? Your mind cannot go beyond 100 pushups; therefore, your body cannot surpass that

number. In fact, you have found a comfort zone and you are unwilling to leave it. There is no pressure, so it feels like home. I've got news for you. When it begins to feel like home, your best is gradually dying away!

When you are no longer under pressure, your mind is no longer attentive – its heightened sensitivity is dulled by a lack of challenge. It begins to lose its ability to function optimally. Here's a quick example: when do you feel more alive and active to do your daily activities; is it when you are a bit hungry or when you are full and satiated? Obviously, when you are a bit hungry, you find the physical vigor and mental alertness to perform your activities well. (Have you considered why many people find it more fulfilling to exercise on empty stomachs, especially in the mornings?) But when you have eaten and are full, your cognitive functions become a bit dull. Your brain simply lulls you to relax or even take a nap. Why? It has reached its climax – there is no more pressure to seek satisfaction, so the next natural thing to do is simply to relax.

In the same vein, when your mind senses that there is no longer any pressure, it dulls you and your best does not come to fore. That is why if you want to grow your mind to the point of being unbeatable, you must welcome pressure. You should cherish the moments when there is pressure because those are the times you come out shining. For those who do not wish to leave their comfort zone, pressure puts them in an uncontrollable situation, but for you, it is a welcomed development and you are more than able to control such situations.

An unbeatable mind:

- Does not panic in the face of pressure; it is always calm, cool, and collected.

- Sees pressure as a stepping stone.
- Shines brighter in the face of adversity.
- Knows the importance of constant growth; therefore, it seeks opportunities to step out of its comfort zone.

Start Counting When You're Tired

Picture an athlete doing 100 pushups and counting from the first pushup. At the hundredth, they are done and move on to something else. Well, that's one way to do 100 pushups. Here's another way: do as many as you can until you are tired, then begin to count from 1. If you can get to 100, you have truly accomplished something worth celebrating. (And I am not just referring to pushups alone). This is a simple tactic to break a previous record. Take yourself to the height where you have been before, then begin to convince your mind that that level is your starting point! This will keep you going when most other people would have quit. It doesn't matter in what area of life you apply this technique - it works all the time.

It is the unconscious programming that kicks in to tell you that you cannot go beyond a certain point. It is your fragile mind that puts up the imaginary barrier and cajoles you into thinking that it is real. And as a matter of fact, your mind can easily come up with concrete evidence to show you how impossible it is to hit your target. And if you are like most people, you will cower in obeisance and accept that limitation.

But if you are tired of being told what you can or cannot do (whether by your fragile mind or from external sources), you will most definitely:

Be the first person in and certainly the last person out.

Continue working and giving it, one more tries even when others have given up or said it can't be done.

Be the one with an incredible work ethic.

There's something liberating when you understand the power of your mind. As much as it shapes your world, it can only do so from the information you feed it. So, if you constantly feed your mind with debilitating thoughts such as, "I can't go any further", "it's just impossible", "no one has been able to do this", etc., your intelligent mind will dutifully surround you with evidence to prove you right. On the flip side, if you honestly think and feel, "it's not over until I succeed", "I know I can do this", "I am built for this", guess what? Those thoughts fuel your mind to create a reality that matches them.

However, you should realize that it takes a considerable amount of time for your mind to be transformed from a fragile state into an unbeatable state, just as it took a long time for your authority figures to (unintentionally) drum mediocrity into you.

Stay Humble... No Matter What!

Did you read the part where I said not to disregard constituted authority? Well, I meant it. If not checked, the feeling of success has a way of making people cocky. And you know what they say - pride comes before a fall.

As much as I want you to have an unbeatable mind (which, by the way, is not negotiable if you want to succeed), you must also develop an attitude to put pride in its rightful place. However, aside from success making people proud, tough situations also have a way of making people rebel against constituted authority.

Your trainer, for example, may put you through rigorous training that will bring you to your breaking point (we all have them). And at that point, you may feel like giving up and walking away. But if you recognize that discipline is not punishment (as discussed earlier in Chapter 2) and accept that your success is the goal, you will most likely embrace the process and humbly learn to develop the habits that are being instilled in you.

Here are a few ways to help you keep your head down no matter what:

- Keep your focus on the result even if the process is unpleasant.
- Pain is temporary; the gain is worth it.
- Get your mind off the pain and your body will feel it less; mind over matter works every time.
- If you are training with others, consider the possibility that you are an inspiration to both your colleagues and your trainer.
- You are growing into an authority in your field, so stay humble so that others are humble towards you too.

As I bring this chapter to a close, let me quickly elaborate on an important point I mentioned in an earlier paragraph. We all have breaking points; I mean, that's why we are humans, right? This book is aimed at making you tough mentally, but I do not intend in any way to make you toughen up to the point of being suicidal. There are some physical strains that are not suitable for everyone.

Recognizing your physical limits and drawing the line at that point will enable you to stay physically safe to accomplish whatever it is you desire. Going beyond your physical limitation is not advised as it may jeopardize your physical health and by extension, your mental health too. Therefore, I strongly urge you to know your physical limits and make your activities fit into your known boundaries. This is not to say you cannot be, do, or have whatever your mind conceives and believes. Always remember this: even though there are physical limits, there are none for the mind!

Chapter 6:
The Hidden Rule to Push Yourself to the Limit

Ever wondered how Navy SEALs are so mentally tough?

And no, they are not superhumans. They are humans like you who have mastered the art of breaking their mental barrier and overcoming their limitations. Thanks to this, they can rise above the boundaries of their flesh and complete any task successfully.

The SEALs believe that no matter how tired you feel, you are still far from your limit and you are still capable of so much more. In short, the feeling of fatigue is the brain's way of shying away from pain.

"It's a way of saying that by drawing on our mental strength we can push through any situation. When the chips are down, tell yourself you have at least 40 percent left in the tank." (Jesse Itzler)

The 40% Rule: Any Scientific Backing?

If you look at the 40% rule critically, you will notice that it is not a rule. Instead, it's another way of saying you are capable of so much more than you think. Hence, when you feel like you have reached your limit, you are a few miles away from your starting point.

Hence, whether we call it the 20%, 30% or 45% rule doesn't matter. What matters is the fact that your mind should be the one to determine how far you go, and not your muscles.

There is a lot of research to support the fact that it is your brain, not your muscles that determines your endurance strength and limit. We have been made to believe that muscles get tired because we physically can't go on any longer. Hence, we are unable to continue our task because we exhausted fuel or the buildup of metabolites – the byproduct of muscle contraction.

Professor Tim Noakes in 1990 revealed that the brain limits your muscle to prevent it from going to exhaustion. (Christian Finn)

In a bid to prevent exhaustion, the brain triggers the distressing signals that it is time to quit. This is when you feel muscle fatigue.

This is your brain restricting you from tapping into your reserve in a bid to make you have the provision in case of an emergency.

The 40% Rule: Key to Unlocking Your Mental Toughness

There is something that separates high performers from ordinary people. High fliers and people we think as superhuman are ordinary people that have learned to overcome the mental barrier many are faced with.

In understanding the 40% rule, it is essential to explain why our brain sometimes holds us back.

Civilization at Breakneck Speed

From the beginning of times, humans have been known to fight to survive, and this has conditioned the brain to do everything it can to keep us alive. In the past, humans mainly fought this way to meet basic living needs, as well as to fight threats, infections, and disease. Our forefathers had a lot of things against them.

However, as the years passed, development began, which translated into a developed quality of life. Our health system makes use of sophisticated technology, and man is not limited in transportation as airplanes can take you just about anywhere.

Many people have access to a quality life, fresh food, and shelter, and this development came at a mighty speed.

The Human's Primitive Brain

This development was quick and beneficial to man. However, our brain could not keep up with the pace. While humans have evolved into the twentieth century, the brain is still in primitive days. So many things our forefathers usually struggled with are now readily available.

Ultimately, this means that humans have more time to worry about other things. Humans now crave to enjoy life, as well as to be recognized and feel fulfilled. Even with this development, we still react instinctively to our environment.

Even if hardly facing any danger, the brain exaggerates the slightest bit of it. This was very useful to our forefathers as it ensured their survival. However, life and society have evolved, but the brain couldn't keep up with this way of life.

Since the brain is lagging in this regard, it is more after our comfort and well-being. It prioritizes comfort and dreads every sign of harm or stress. The brain has been programmed to restrict and flee at the slightest tendency of risk and danger all in a bid to keep us alive.

This has made man limited, which manifests itself when we run a marathon but stop halfway because we feel like we can't go on. You can also feel this when trying intermittent fasting in a bid to lose weight, but every fiber of your being keeps screaming that you are going die. You give up on everything you set your heart to, even though you already overcame the reluctance of starting.

In a bid to keep us alive, our brain encourages us to give up for short-term comfort.

The 40% Rule

It is impossible to completely overcome the resistance from our brain when we set out to start a task that seems confusing. But the good news is that we can gradually rise against it, nipping it in the bud with every hard task we undergo. So, you can train your brain to recognize and get over the mental barrier that keeps you stagnant.

The 40% rule is quite simple. When you think you are done, when you feel you have used up all your capacity, when you feel like you lack the will and mental strength to keep going – you have just exhausted 40% of your ability. In other words, when many people get to the point of quitting, only 40% of their physical and mental strength has been exhausted. Many people are full of great things and capable of so much more. Hence, when you realize that you still have so much left in your tank, it does seem horrible to throw in the towel, doesn't it?

The 40% principle was the effort of Jesse Itzler, a Californian billionaire entrepreneur in his life-changing book – 'Living with a Seal.' The 40% rule originates from a time when Jesse and a set of other people had a 24-hour race to complete. During this endurance race, Jesse met with David Goggin's, a US Navy SEAL who chose to run the entire marathon solo.

Despite all odds, David resisted the urge to quit and kept going. He was able to complete the race even with a broken bone, which fascinated Jesse. Inspired by his unique mental strength, Jesse wondered how he pulled through. In a quest to know his secret, he asked David to be his mentor. David agreed, on the condition that Jesse will do everything he is asked without exception.

After a month, David moved to go live with Jesse and the Itzler's. This led Jesse to discover things he never knew or believed he was capable of. With David as his mentor, he was able to do 100 pull-ups when he thought he was capable of just eight. David put him through many crazy things that led Jesse to conclude that everyone is capable of so much more.

Training the Brain

The fact many people need to understand is that when you feel like you have given it everything you've got, you haven't. Yes, this is difficult, but to develop your mental strength, you've got to ignore those pesky warning signals from your brain and subject yourself to discomfort. With time, you can learn and train yourself to push through any task set before you.

When you train your brain, you should have three things in mind. The effort to overcome the inertia, the firm determination to block out that little pesky voice asking you to quit and the patience to keep doing what you set out to do.

Whenever you are on the verge of giving up, bear in mind that these are false signals from the brain to avoid stress. Be strong enough to resist it.

Bear in mind that the resistance will come. When it does, be mindful of it and take it as a clue that you are far from doing even half of what you are capable of.

Many of our limitations come from ourselves, and we are capable of way more than we think. One thing you have got to know about the 40% rule is that it must be in your subconscious. Walk with it, remember it whenever you are at the edge of giving up, and draw strength from it to push past your mental barrier. Also, this is just not about sports or physical activities. This applies to every area of our life – work, relationships, restrictions, etc.

Always remember, the human mind can either be your biggest asset or your largest undoing. The ball is in your court.

The 40% Rule: Developing Mental Toughness

The one secret to being resilient, to keep going despite all odds, and to persevere and give any task an extra push is to develop your mental toughness. This will keep you going, irrespective of things in life meant to dissuade you from your path/goal. While we acknowledge that developing mental toughness is not easy, it is possible. We will give you some tactics to build resilience in preparation for bullets and knocks life throws at you.

Before we dive into that, it is important to understand mental toughness.

What is Mental Toughness?

Mental toughness is the ability to persevere and keep going despite adversity and hardship. Mental toughness is what will allow you to keep your eyes on your goal despite all the difficulties you may be facing. Many times, we have high expectations and expect things to go how we want. When this doesn't happen, many people who lack mental toughness are quick to throw in the towel.

However, with mental toughness, you get to learn from your mistakes, so you can make a one and get back up without lamenting over the mess and the psychological devastation of failing. It is mental toughness that gives you the fuel and zeal to keep going when life throws stones at you and everything seems overwhelming.

You should see mental toughness as that tiny voice that motivates you against the will of your flesh. It is that personal encouragement that tells you to do just a little more and that encourages you to keep going when it gets tough and seems impossible.

Manage Your Expectations

To build resilience to the things that come your way, you have got to be careful of your expectations. When your expectations are not managed adequately, you may feel surprised and feel like everything is out of your control.

When they lack control, people tend to worry and become anxious. This ultimately affects your motivation, and this could affect your mental strength. By managing your expectations, you become flexible, ready, and able to adapt to any situation. This is the foundation for a healthy mental strength.

People with high mental strength have developed their ability to remain rigid and unchanged in the face of adversity. These are people that have learned to adapt when situations don't go as planned with the flexibility to seek other ways to tackle what is before them.

It is not about just rolling with the punches; instead, it is about devising ways to take a swing. It is high time you understand that many things will happen that will be out of your control. However, the one thing you can control is your reaction. Always look at situations from a different perspective. If your vision is already tinted with the shade of instant emotional response, you will not be able to objectively understand and see things in their true color. Rather, if you have the time, wait for a couple of minutes before responding. Many people instantly react to an issue without even fully understanding the matter. Be sure to understand any case before you, then put the pieces together.

The following are tricks to becoming flexible and managing your expectations.

Redefine Your Reality

The way to keep your expectation realistic is to understand them. While we have no control over surprises, a good idea to prepare ourselves is to anticipate the likely outcome of an issue. When you understand your expectations, you can be honest with yourself and form realistic ones. Therefore, it is a bad idea to rely on possibilities or to put so much faith in your expectations. This sets you up for disappointment when things don't go as planned.

The ability to anticipate and accept outcomes will make you healthy, prepared, and unmoved by surprises when they come.

Don't Let Emotions Get the Best of You

While it is an excellent idea to be in touch with your emotions, at times, they can also cloud your judgment. Most times, emotions do not allow people to approach situations objectively. Developing emotional resilience is critical in fighting through difficult conditions.

According to the 40% rule, it is emotions that make people give up quickly rather than keep going. A simple way to build and improve on your emotional resilience is to own whatever situation you find yourself in, rather than run towards comfort – and yes, this is the approach most people opt for, as it is the easy way out!

Taking the easy way out means never getting out of your comfort zone. This will rob you of vital lessons and of the benefits of perseverance. There is no way you can know how much you know until you try to know. However, if you don't try to know, if you don't give yourself the chance of proving that you can do it, there is no way you can know.

Form the habit of getting comfortable in stressful situations as this will help deal with stress. *According to the SEALs, you must get comfortable being uncomfortable.*

To keep going when things get tough is the boost you need to stay calm when things go haywire. While being in touch with your emotion is right, be sure to be in control.

Always Be in Touch with Your Motivation

Without the needed motivation, managing your expectations and taking charge of your emotions will not get you far. Whatever task you are faced with, you need inner motivation to keep going. To push through in the face of that difficult task, you need the motivation to keep going.

- To become motivated, you have got to ask yourself "why?"
- Why am I doing this?
- Why do I need to push through?

The answers to these questions are key to understanding why you should keep going. However, bear in mind that your answers shouldn't be "because I have to", because in the face of something challenging, you do not always have a choice.

Instead, set a specific goal and consider a third party or someone that depends on you. A person may be trying to lose weight to be more attractive, so they may give reasons like:

- Because I want to feel attractive
- Because I want to avoid diseases that come with obesity
- Because my family and friends need me alive

Knowing why it is important to see something through makes facing it easier. It doesn't stop here though, because you must break the barriers that come with this. This happens through strong willpower and mental strength. Building these up takes time but is possible.

When you accomplish a small task, you get to boost your willpower, leading to an improvement in confidence. This helps you realize how much you can do and how far you can go, ultimately helping you believe in yourself.

Willpower is said to be inexhaustible, and in fact, you have as much willpower as you think you have. With this, you have got to challenge yourself and access your motivation, and surmounting obstacles will be easier than you think.

Come to Terms with Delayed Gratification

One of the best success strategies is accepting things as they are and learning to accept failure. However, it doesn't come easy as it requires mental toughness.

Being mentally tough encompasses many things. One of them is the ability to delay gratification or to not jump at instant gratification. Always be mindful of the fact that nothing good comes easy. As a result, if you can persevere, work hard, and patiently wait, you will get the grasp of what mental toughness is about.

Mistakes will happen along the way, but do not dwell on them. Things might not go the way you want, but with time and patience, you can accomplish what you set your heart to.

Mental toughness requires denying yourself, telling yourself no, and developing the patience to stand by your decision.

You will be faced with a couple of things that are not worth your time. However, never let go of the mindset that whatever comes your way, you can see it all the way through.

It is important to note that mental toughness does not come overnight. You have got to be determined, patient and consciously strive towards rising against all odds. Equipping yourself to handle all the horrible blows life throws at you comes back to developing mental toughness. This happens via reasonable expectations, true motivation, and getting hold of your emotions.

Chapter 7:
How to Create Confidence when Humiliated

Many people are of the opinion that some people are born with confidence and that these few lucky people have this inherent gift and can walk into a room and take charge. People think that they naturally draw people towards them as a result of their charisma and self-confidence.

However, I must disprove that. Confidence is a skill and quality that comes with practice. In short, if you are the timid person ever, you can take actionable steps to build your self-confidence and lead people. With constant effort and practice, you can take steps to improve your confidence to lead.

Besides being a leader, self-confidence is a terrific quality that will set you apart. People are naturally drawn to confident people as they tend to have the charm and magic to command others. As crucial as self-confidence is, many people see it as a difficult task. However, a lack of confidence could make one terrible at being a leader, whatever field they're in.

This explains why people find it difficult to invest in an idea being aired by a fidgety, nervous, and timid dude. While on the other hand, someone who is knowledgeable, holds his head high, admits his ignorance, and answers your entire question brilliantly will not find it difficult to turn prospects into customers.

Confident people make others sure, and therefore it is an essential attribute for a leader. Besides, to be successful as a leader, you have got to be able to gain the confidence of other people.

Building confidence as a leader does not need to be a daunting task. With the right effort, you can build and learn faith, which is well worth the effort.

What Is Self-Confidence?

There are two significant factors that determine self-confidence: self-efficacy and self-esteem.

The process of mastering skills, setting goals and seeing them to completion, and achieving dreams in yourself and even in other people is a vital key to gaining self-efficacy. In other words, this confidence stems from the fact that focusing on developing and mastering a field or area will help you succeed. This is what gives people the motivation and challenge to accept and face a seemingly impossible task to the end, despite many setbacks.

Self-efficacy goes hand in hand with the idea of self-esteem. Self-esteem is the school of thought that we have control of things that happen in our life and can accept it. However, some of this is due to the assurance that people we know and love such as friends and families approve of us, which is usually out of our control. Also, part of it comes from the fact that we know we are skilled at what we do, are at our best, and can achieve whatever we set our heart to.

There are many things that you can do to gain the confidence to lead, from building your skills, to affirmation, to positive thinking. This is what this chapter seeks to explore. And, when you are done reading this chapter, I hope you understand that self-confidence and the confidence you need to be a leader is a skill you can learn. It is not a skill restricted to a group of people.

Building Self-Confidence to Lead

How do you develop your confidence to lead? How will you build the charisma that sets you out as an exceptional leader whom others are naturally drawn towards?

While there is no quick fix or secret formula, it is possible. With diligence, dedication, and determination, you can build self-confidence which will translate to success in everything you set your heart to. The best part is that the tips and tricks to building confidence automatically set you on the path to success. You should not forget that confidence comes from tangible achievements that stay with you for life.

To build the confidence to lead, we will focus on three metaphors and provide you with as many tips as possible.

Step1: Getting Set for The Journey

To develop the confidence to lead, you have got to be set for the journey. In other words, consider your starting point and your destination. It is not all about physical preparation alone, but mental preparation as well. You must do a lot of things to prepare yourself for the journey ahead.

The following are some steps to get set for the journey:

Don't Lose Sight of Your Achievements

In other words, create an achievement journal. And if you will be leading a team, allow stubborn projects you led your team to inspire you. Deals you were able to close and prospects you successfully turned to clients etc. are achievements that can keep you going as a leader. It can even be as simple as an idea that changed the course of your business.

When the going gets tough, get in the habit of coming back to these achievements and draw strength from them. Look at them every morning and let them inspire you to do better. The power that comes from knowing you are successful is enough to give you the needed zeal to keep pushing in the face of discouragement. By doing so, you gradually build your confidence.

Ensure to update this achievement log from time to time. Whenever you achieved a goal that you have set, proudly engrave it in gold on your record and add tougher ones.

Reflect on Your Strength

This technique is like a SWOT analysis to consider who you are and where you are headed. Still drawing inspiration from your achievement journal, try and analyze your strengths and weaknesses. To get honest opinions, asking your friends and family is an excellent idea.

Consider the Things That Matter

In your quest to build your confidence to lead, you have got to prioritize things that matter as well as your goals with the team. You have got to set achievable goals, in your interest as well as the interest of the people you are leading. This is one of the ways to truly gain confidence.

When you set goals, you establish your targets and judge your success based on reaching such targets. Also, allow your SWOT analysis to guide you. In other words, capitalize on your strengths, reduce your weaknesses, bank on your opportunities, and control your threats.

Take Control of Your Mind

This is where you have got to get your mind in order. Be sure to identify those pesky little voices in the back of your head that damage your self-confidence. Try and think positively.

Make it a habit to employ the power of positive mental imagery to create sharp images of how it will feel like to reach your goal. Imagine the satisfaction that comes from this. Draw strength from it as there is a sense of possibility that comes from this that makes even the hardest goal seem achievable.

Commit Yourself to Success

To develop your confidence to lead, the final piece of the first puzzle is to commit yourself to the goals you have set. In other words, promise yourself you can do it and that you will give it all it takes to complete what you set your heart to.

While this might lead to self-doubts, don't ignore them. Take note of them and rationally challenge them. Identify the reason for the uncertainty and devise strategies to counter them. If your doubts come from genuine concerns, ensure to come up with additional procedures to remove them.

Final Tips on Getting Set for The Journey

Developing the confidence to lead should always be about balance. There are two extremes; on one side, there are people that suffer from low confidence, while on other, some may come off as overconfident.

Being underconfident will limit you as you will hardly come out of your comfort zone and will not stretch yourself, robbing you of knowing what you are capable of. On the other hand, excessive confidence could come back and hurt you as well because you overstretch yourself and the team and bank on things beyond your capacity, making you crash.

You have got to get things right and make sure to balance your self-confidence. This should be based on your real strengths. Just the perfect amount of self-confidence to lead will help you take calculated risks, stretch yourself to achieve your limits, and not view tasks as insurmountable.

Step 2: Launch Out

This is where you start gradually, adding bricks on top of bricks to your wall of confidence, getting closer to your goal with every step you take. Every passing day, you focus on an essential task and enjoy the easy wins and small goals that add up to the big one. You are on the path to success, improving your confidence as you go on.

In launching out, the following are tips that gear you towards building your confidence:

Gather the Essential Knowledge and Experience

With your target in mind, you have got to identify the right skill you need to make it a reality. The confidence to be a leader comes from mastering the required expertise to lead your team towards reaching their goals.

We are not talking about sketchy skills just to get the job done. It is about acquiring the skill that adds to your wealth of knowledge and experience. This doesn't mean just coming up with a 'good-enough' solution. This is something that sets you out as knowledgeable. The feeling of being knowledgeable alone can give you the needed boost to lead effectively.

Don't Forget the Basics

Developing the confidence needed to lead is not about trying something clever or trying to impress. It is not about being perfect either, as confident people own up to their mistakes. Hence, in your journey towards perfection, be sure to enjoy the simple things and take pride in their success. Doing this well will add an additional feather to your cap of confidence.

Celebrate Small Goals and Achievements

In the first step, we spoke about the importance of small goals. Be sure not to lose the habit of setting small goals. Besides, even a so-called big goal is a collection of small goals. Also, setting goals should not be a challenging task.

It is about having them, achieving them, and celebrating them. With time, this forms your success story.

Be in Control of Your World

Never at any moment let go of strong positive mental images. Make them the fuel to keep you on track of achieving your needed desire. Be sure to always tap into the tremendous potential that comes with positive thinking.

Besides, to develop confidence, you need to get better at handling failure. One of the things that sets a confident person apart is the fact that they own up to their mistakes and shortcomings, which is bound to happen when trying something new. Errors should be steps on the path towards progress.

Step 3: Gear Towards Success

Before getting to the third stage, you should have felt your confidence to lead building up. Many of the things you set your heart to in the previous step should already be done. Hence, there should be enough success to serve as motivation.

This is not a clue to stop but to keep going. Set bigger and harder goals and be sure to always be on your toes. Make more commitments and seek new areas to apply the skills you have learned.

Be sure not to allow overconfidence to eat you up. Resist the urge to take on a task in order to prove your capabilities to your followers.

Keep stretching yourself, but make sure you do it gradually. This is part of the building block you need to add to your wall of self-confidence.

The most essential skill you need to improve to gain more confidence to be a leader is setting goals, so make sure to utilize this tested skill.

Chapter 8:
How Navy SEALS Stay in Control in Any Situation

If you aspire to become more resilient or just extraordinary in everything you do, you must investigate the life of a Navy SEAL and learn from it. There is a wide range of lessons to learn from these people who are always ready to take on the toughest challenges whenever needed. Even though you do not intend to go through the same rigors as the SEALs, you may want to look out for the things that set them aside from other US Armed Forces and of course, Armed Forces across the globe.

In the past, several members of the elite group have shared their experience and knowledge of the ways people excelled beyond their physical prowess both at training camps and in the line of duty. Therefore, for everyone who wishes to improve, it is necessary to learn lessons from these special forces, follow their leads, and watch how much better they are going to become.

Mental Toughness and Resilience

Winston Churchill once advised that when you are going through hell, you should keep going. This is a very valuable piece of advice. Navy SEALs are the toughest in the world because they have successfully walked through hell. This is because, over time, they have developed mental toughness. This is important for every aspect of life as it is a well-known/effective tool to achieve long-term success. All that matter is having the ability to keep going when the going gets extremely tough. You see, in today's world of smartphones, automated procedures, and artificial intelligence, people tend to chicken out at the slightest difficulty. Therefore, what sets one apart from the rest is one's ability to cultivate mental agility and resilience. This helps place one's head high up in the air to become a pacesetter/forerunner of another people's success

To create a state of mental toughness, the first step that SEALs goes through is a sort of mental segmentation. Imagining that they must eat an elephant, SEALs segment their challenge into parts so that they can gradually eat one part after the other. This works in real life scenarios, so whatever you are faced with, it is important to break it down into surmountable parts. Take marathoners for example; instead of creating a mental visualization of the entire race, they take it one lap at a time, slowing down and going faster when they should, and picking up all the strength left in them as they get close to the finish line. If they approached every single step of the race with the same energy, they would either be too exhausted to get the finish line, or too slow to get to it. In real life situations, when you have a mountain-sized task, break it down into smaller rocks and approach them one after the other. Avoid thinking of the task in its entirety as this may be discouraging. However, you should try to fit the segmented tasks into a 24-hour schedule.

Another technique employed by SEALs is to create a mental picture of success. This serves as self-motivation. By visualizing success, you sort of get a feel of what success is like. While at it, you are forced to envisage all the things you should do and all the steps you need to take to achieve this success. While doing so, make sure you put all your senses to work. Also, make sure your mental picture of success is as real as possible, as you do not want to build castles in the air. Try to not picture yourself failing as much as you can, and rather continuously picture yourself succeeding effortlessly. Think about the consequences of possible failure. You will not want to disappoint your loved one, so picture their faces as they hear the news of your failure. Also, consider the embarrassment that comes with failure, then play all these images in your head again from time to time until success is a reality. Whenever you must get through a difficult phase, think of what it will feel like to come out of it successfully, and use that as your motivating factor.

Talk Positively to Yourself

One of the characteristics of SEALS is the ability to stay calm in the face of danger. According to research, the brain is always active, and it is estimated to say about 300 to 1000 words per minute. To this effect, when you seem to be in the face of danger, the brain goes to work, suggesting an avalanche of 'how's' and 'what ifs. So, the good thing is that you can control what goes on in your head. Like the Navy SEAL, always make sure there is no room for negative thoughts in your head.

There are a whole lot of things that SEALs are not allowed to do, and one of them is to panic. Even when underwater and with their oxygen mask suddenly yanked off, instead of panicking, a SEAL works to find ways to restore the mask. When the brain goes into danger mode and wants to tell you that you are about to die, the mind of a Navy SEAL goes into positive thoughts and tells himself that survival is the only option, and that optimism is key. This is in sharp contrast to the mind of a pessimist. A pessimist always reminds himself of the magnitude of a problem and convinces himself that a bad situation is going to last forever, or perhaps that such situations are a universal phenomenon, like, "trust issues are universal; no one can be trusted". Also, they find fault in themselves in everything; "I am just not good at hiking". A Navy SEAL's mind sees positivity at all times; "Oh! This won't last forever, I'll overcome it", bad things are there are for a reason; "if I can't trust a person or people, it is for a reason" and finally, a SEAL doesn't fault himself for every failure; the fact that he was unable to complete a task is because he probably missed a step, not because he isn't good at it. When talking to yourself, it is important to rid your mind of all forms of pessimism. Remember that success is what you are in for, and negative thoughts drown you faster than you can imagine.

A SEAL constantly tells himself that so many people have passed the test in the past and those people are not better than them. Every minute of their training comes with rigorous mental and physical tests, so they constantly must give themselves positive talks to keep their eyes on the goal and to never give up. This can be you in every aspect of your life. Tests and trials will certainly come your way, but you always must tell yourself that you are not the worse off person in life. So, as the strongest among the many strong people alive, you will excel.

Control Your Emotions

There are times when our emotions seem to rush in like a flood and at such times, we are likely to lose control of all our senses. These emotions may be a result of stress and as soon as they hit, our major stress hormones - adrenaline, cortisol, and norepinephrine - provide us with a boost of energy. However, there is only so much these hormones can take. When they are elevated for a long period, it becomes impossible to switch to relaxation mode. Sleeping becomes a task, motivations fall to an all-time low, and the immune system has a tough time functioning. In such situations, the SEALs apply a solution known as 4 by 4 of 4. Here is how it works: breathe out for four seconds, breathe in for four seconds, then repeat it another four minutes.

This may look familiar as so many experts like yogis have been doing this for quite a long time. The truth is that our bodies have effects on our brains and vice versa. When the body is stressed, the brain sends signals that tell you to take some time off. It gets to a point where the brain literally shuts down as a result of stress. This simple breathing exercise helps you switch your stress hormones off and prepare the body for relaxation. When you get to the point of raging emotions, the best thing you can do is to stop everything you are doing. Remind yourself of the fact that you will not achieve much if your emotions are not right so as often as you can, take a moment off to do the 4 by 4 of 4. If you are having a bad day at work, pause, breathe and continue. Maybe you are an introvert that is faced with the herculean task of addressing a crowd. Once you get on that stage, it may seem like your tongue is stuck to the roof of your mouth. Well, you may not have the time to do the last four, but the first fours will certainly work magic in calming your nerves. Breathe in and out and notice how your tension eases.

Set Goals

At some point, all your muscles and nerves will scream at you to quit and will even threaten to break down if you don't. At such times, you need all the motivation you can get to keep going. Goals are very good motivating factors. Navy SEALs like to set achievable goals, which are sometimes small, but they are always enough to keep them going at tough times. For a Navy SEAL, during training, making it to the next minute may be a very difficult task as they have tons of hurdles to cross while the clock is ticking. Their small goals, however, could be to make it to lunch or dinner at the training camp so when they are underwater, they must keep reminding themselves that it is impossible to quit or die as they must eat lunch or dinner at the camp, not elsewhere, and certainly not as a dead man. This may be an extremely inconsequential phenomenon for the other man, but for the SEAL, it is important to keep him going. When they achieve their goals, they set new ones which are often a step ahead of the former. The goal is to keep improving and keep getting better.

For you, these goals are also very important. Keep a note of the things you want to achieve and make sure you don't relent until you achieve them. Track your success as there is no better motivation than seeing yourself succeed. Like the Navy SEAL, when you have achieved a goal, set your sights higher by setting new ones. Make sure you prepare yourself to achieve your goals by creating a visual picture of the journey towards achieving these goals.

Visualization

The task ahead of you may seem so humongous that you may already have some doubts about it. Well, since it is ahead, you may not know what it feels like now, but you can prepare yourself to know what to expect and what not to. This will be made easy by simply creating a mental picture of the whole process. This way, you will have already envisaged the possible twists and turns that you are most likely to encounter. As you are creating this picture, make room for eventualities so that you are not thrown off your feet at any point while carrying out the task. This can be done by simply closing your eyes and meditating for a few minutes. Picture what is ahead of you, then walk yourself through each step of it. It may sound silly, but the best of the best does it and it absolutely works. SEALs are taught to do this a lot by having a mental rehearsal of the activities that are to come, then visualizing themselves succeeding in those activities. However, be careful not to merely fantasize about these things because this will mean that you will not see any obstacles in your journey. Bring the possible obstacles into the picture and visualize yourself surpassing them.

Fantasies are a known killer of motivation as they do not really give you the energy you need to undertake the task ahead of you. After forming a mental picture of your task, you must find ways to take it to the next level like a professional, and that brings us to the next technique:

Make Use of Simulations

While it is a great idea to visualize the task ahead, it is equally good to take some mock exercises to align yourself with the things you are going to undergo. The good thing about visualization is that is very mobile, so you can do it anywhere and everywhere.

It has been discovered that SEALs don't just visualize. It has been said that before the Navy SEALs raided Osama Bin-Laden's house, they created replicas of the location, so their training was tailored towards the things they were likely to face. Like the US Navy SEAL team 6 on the 11th of May 2011, you too can create mental simulations of the exercises ahead of you. If you are going to have a presentation, for example, create a small supportive group and practice in front of them. If according to your mental picture, you are going to answer questions from members of your audience, ask those in your small group to ask you tough questions. Treat those questions as the real deal and answer them as though your success depends on it. This way, you will have gotten yourself acquainted with most parts of your exercise.

Think of Small Victories

Some days can be so bad that it feels like everything is going wrong. Remember, the power of positive thoughts will give you more strength than you may be able to sum up on your own. However, on the days where you seem to be losing it, what you are expected to do is to think of those small but highly consequential victories of yours.

The day may have started off as every other day, but you stepped out of the house and realized that you must have lost your wallet. To make things worse, it suddenly began to rain and now, your phone is drenched in water. Also, you got to work late and now, you are going to get queried. Well, how worse could your day have gone? Maybe it is time to look at the bright side and think about the days when you were the champion of your workplace because you single-handedly completed a task that shaped the fate of the entire company. Remind yourself of the fact that you are still that champion and that the bad day is only temporary. Tomorrow is just another day to show off your greatness. You may also want to think smaller; maybe the office scenario is not for you, depending on what you do. Now, think of the times you said a joke that made everyone laugh; maybe it is time to be your own savior by telling yourself the same joke or even more, to win a smile. Also, you could think about the many times you made your daughter's day by buying her candy on your way home from work. Picture her reaction - does it warm your heart? Maybe it is time to get another heart-melting reaction from your darling little daughter. We know you have lost your wallet but what greater victory is there than to go out of your way to make the one that means so much to you happy? Think of how happy you will be to make her happy. To Navy SEALs, this is another way to get themselves to keep moving in the race of life that seems to be filled with perpetual adversaries.

The thought of small victories lifts one's morale and high morale will propel you to push forward to even higher morale. This is basically the stepping stone to victory, so if you seem to be having a not so pleasant day, you should consider your small wins instead of counting the big losses.

Stay Away from Bad Stuff

The fact that Navy SEALs undergo the toughest training in the US military makes them qualified to take on anyone at any time. It also means that they stand tall as one of the most prestigious arms of the US military. However, this does not mean that they are ready to take up arms at the slightest provocation. Navy SEALs are thought to avoid bad situations before they happen until fighting becomes inevitable. People generally think that a SEAL's first reaction would be to take up arms. This is untrue. They only use their arms as a last resort. This is a very potent technique that should be applied to everyone's dealings. Try to avoid bad situations as much as possible, no matter how strong you may think you are. Even though you may have what it takes to handle the situation, if it is bad, avoid it as much as you can. You should not waste your time around bad vibes that can be avoided.

Be Humble

As strong as Navy SEALs are, they are a humble lot and in so many cases, as already explained with the previous technique, they learn not to wield their strength. A SEAL team leader is said to always recognize the fact that he is not the solution to every problem. Once he begins to place himself in front of every problem, he is said to be heading towards failure. It is against this background that delegation comes in. Also, they are humble enough to accept their faults when things go wrong, to accept constructive criticism, to listen when they should and call for help when it is necessary. This does not mean they are weak, and it doesn't diminish their leadership status; if anything, it makes them better leaders. Humility is a technique that has built successful leaders across all walks of life. Certainly, this technique is not restricted to leaders alone. Followers also always need to be humble enough to know and accept their position.

You never want to rub shoulders with your superiors or anyone at all in whatever situation, so humility always comes in handy. This is a great way to eliminate stress.

Box Breathing

This technique called box breathing works to keep you cool and it is called that way because it has four simple steps, each in four seconds (a square). This technique can be practiced anytime and anywhere you feel the need to relax, whether you are on a battlefront, in an exam hall, at a seminar, or simply reading a tweet. It only takes sixteen seconds to complete one circle and you can keep repeating it until you feel relaxed. For the SEAL, on the other hand, it is advised to do this technique for five minutes. Here is a step by step rundown of this technique:

Breathe in for four seconds: you are expected to expel every atom of air from your lungs before you breathe in. Once done, begin to inhale and make sure you take in all the air you can to fill your lungs to their full capacity.

Hold your breath for another four seconds - at this point, you are no longer expected to take in any air, and you must ensure that no air escapes from your lungs.

Exhale for four seconds: now, gradually expel the air from your lungs for four seconds. Make sure you can get all the air out of your lungs.

Leave your lungs empty for four seconds - you may be tempted to inhale right after you let out all the air from your lungs, but please don't. Wait another four seconds before you take in air again.

Just like the 4 by 4 for 4, this is just another technique that will work perfectly to keep you calm in the face of great trouble. Give it a try.

Find the Most Important Moment

In SEAL training, one of the toughest routines is training to attack enemy ships. During this training, a candidate is left underwater on his own and must swim to attack an enemy ship. The ship is built in a way where you get no light from the moon or from any nearby street lights, and ambient lights are also blocked. They are simply left in the dark with their instinct to go and attack a ship by themselves, approaching it from the bottom. The candidate is meant to go under the ship to find the center line and the deepest part of the ship. The most difficult part of the mission is described by some that have passed through the training, as the darkest part. However, it is also seen as the most important part, so it is very important to get everything right to know when and how to strike. These phases exist in everyone's life and like the Navy SEAL, it is important to not only strike at the right time but to also not miss the catch.

Be Aware of your Surroundings

This might come off as a very basic technique but thanks to mobile devices and gadgets, that is not the case anymore. Being aware of one's surrounding is another way in which SEALs can excel. Once you step into an environment, take note of the tiny little details so that you know when something changes. Any change at all may be a sign of possible danger so in order not to be caught unaware, Navy SEALs are trained to always be alert by knowing their surroundings. Whether in an office or in a public place, try to get your head up from your computer or mobile phone and study what is going on around you. You may notice that everyone has suddenly gone quiet or that people are suddenly beginning to avoid some things. Asides from people, you may also find out that the position of a thing has changed, or a part of the room has become cooler than it used to be. Knowing the reason for these changes will be enough to tell you to either run or stay. This is a very simple technique that you should imbibe.

Chapter 9: How the Extraordinary Stay Extraordinary

Reading this book indicates that you are interested in mental toughness, but let me ask you this, do you really know what it is, what it entails, and what it requires? Some people are born with this mental toughness while some are not, so they will need to work harder to develop it. The good thing about mental toughness is that there are things you can do to improve it, but are you ready for it?

Getting ready for mental toughness is a common challenge faced by a lot of athletes of all sports, parents, performers, and coaches. Fully developing your mental strength requires a lot of skills training which is the key to achieving the goals set before you, and this training is always where we find it difficult to keep up; we might get stuck and give up in the process and end up going back to where we started.

The truth is, training your mental strength to its full potential will benefit you when you put more work to it. But how do you develop this mental strength? First, let us define what mental toughness is.

What Is Mental Toughness?

Now, for easier understanding, I will define mental toughness in two parts:

Mental toughness is the ability to get into a certain zone of action and as a reward for doing that, your performance gets to its peak when you need it the most.

Also, it is the grit or resilience that you use to push through the adversity you are facing in order to achieve success.

Mental toughness is often associated with sportsmen, but it applies to life in general and developing it would do everyone a great deal of good.

Is Mental Toughness Important?

Maybe you are already in the process of training for your mental process, or you are about to embark in the journey towards this and want to take a step back because are beginning to doubt whether it is important for you. Well, the obvious truth is that building your mental toughness can help you separate the good from the great.

Have you ever asked yourself why the world's top performers always retain their titles and take the trophies home? Can you figure out why they are always winners and wouldn't want to give room for any kind of mistakes as they always try to achieve their goals?

If you have asked yourself this before, you are not alone. I have studied and even worked with different sportsmen from different parts of the world and they all have the same secret to winning. They all state that mental toughness is critical in order to win.

Let's create a scenario here: you are taking part in a very important competition and you begin to choke of fear, and anxiety walks in, you get scared and switch to a zone where you are not supposed to be. To take on such a competition, you need enough mental toughness.

As a sportsman, the first rule of sports psychology is that you need mental toughness to achieve top performance. Getting mentally tough is not about your physical abilities. Successfully getting mentally tough borders on changing how you think. It requires an everyday discipline and a daily effort.

The greatest challenge faced by individuals that want to achieve mental toughness is that they tend to dwell in the past and never progress on their journey to becoming mentally tough. Humans are bound to go through changes all the time and sometimes, these may be positive changes, but it happens to everyone, even those that seem to be doing very well at the highest levels

Getting mentally tough will make you uncomfortable, but the discomfort is an important piece that will help you build your mental toughness. Whether you are a sportsman, a SEAL candidate, a business professional, or anything else, you will have to go through this discomfort in order to achieve that toughness, but at the end of the day, it is all worth it. Now, you know how important mental toughness is to become a winner.

The 5 Steps to Developing Mental Strength

After doing lots of research, reading quite several memoirs from different ex-SEALS, and speaking to a handful of world winners, I have come to realize that building mental toughness requires work and there are steps to take in order to achieve this.

I have carefully taken the time to put these simple techniques down, and they have been proven to work for a lot of people. Now, the question is - are you ready? If you are, read on to learn simple techniques that will help you build your mental toughness.

Each technique I have written here comes with an explanation and a practical application to a person's real life.

Step 1: Take the Bull by the Horn; Take Little Steps

If you are asking yourself how the hell you are going to take a bull by the horn, well, we don't mean this literally. It means getting involved one step at a time without letting distractions in. When you are faced with a daunting task like a marathon with many competitors beside you, you can get scared, feel that fear, and end up stopping before you even start, and you don't want that.

As a sportsman, the solution to this fear is segmentation. You should slowly divide your tasks into more workable parts by taking your challenges one step at a time. I know you might have often heard the cliché saying, "one step at a time", but it always works, so why not try it?

This technique is employed by many triathletes and ultra-marathoners. They focus on their immediate objective, the next point of achievement, and block all distractions throughout the entire race.

Application: You should break your daunting tasks into immediate little goals. In order to make it less stressful and boring, they should preferably fit in a few hours. When you do this, focus on completing each part one at a time instead of facing all tasks at once.

This technique should help you attempt the task instead of getting overwhelmed with the fear of the unknown and eventually avoiding it.

Step 2: Focused Visualization

You might be wondering how you can picture success when you are not successful yet. Well, you will get the answer to this question after reading all about this technique and you will know that it will help a great deal in building your mental toughness.

A footballer always imagines scoring a goal before he eventually scores it, and a basketballer will visualize free throws and will later find out that his mental picture of the free throw was somewhat accurate, after making the basket. Why not create that illusion? Why not see yourself doing it? Why not make visualizations come to reality?

I have come to realize that good visualization gives people the following qualities:

- Detailed, vivid, and sharp senses.
- The actualization of your imagination.

Positive imagery

By now, you should know that the secret to happiness is success as it brings happiness along with it. Achieving success involves using the full power of our minds. Since our mind has the power to create and destroy forces of the world, we should use it to our advantage. You can use it to create wonderful things you have dreamed of, but also to take it all away.

If you haven't been making use of visualization, it can be simple for you to get your hands on it, but it can prove daunting too. The question now is; how do you know what you are doing is visualizing or how do you get it right? At one point or the other, you might have been involved in the use of imagination to fantasize about what you like. When you were a kid, you used your imaginary power to daydream about how you would like your future to be, as well as other things.

You should now have a clear picture of what imagination entails and how you can use it. Not everyone can see through their mind's eye but if you can do this, you are at an advantage because imagination comes with its benefits.

If a high-rated Navy SEAL is quietly sitting in the corner of a room before his mission, what do you think he is imagining while seated? The success of his mission or fear of failure? Well, what he is doing there is called focused visualization. This visualization is called focused because it can be controlled, empowered, and fixed at a specific target.

Now, we will be looking at two forms of focused visualization that will help you build your mental toughness as you go.

Performance Imagery

Performance imagery is a form of focused visualization that can be used to develop mental strength for a mission or skill set. If you want to embark on a mission, visualize your plan on how to get your target and keep going over the plan in your mind's eye. You can slow things down in order to make sure you are using the right technique and to ensure it is effective in battle.

Using this technique will allow you to analyze errors and correct them, maintain your skills, increase your confidence, improve your techniques, and simulate your various alternative responses.

When practicing the performance imagery technique, you can add subtle body movements with your eyes closed - this will strengthen the connection between the mind and body and allow the internal visualization to be more prevailing.

Future Imagery

Sometimes, how you see yourself is different from how others see you, whether positively or negatively. However, what if I told you that there was a way to hold a powerful image of who you would like to be in the present as well as in the future?

As a Navy Seal, black belt, senator or firefighter, if you can support your mental vision with action, take away negativity, and fuel what you have envisioned with strong belief, desire, and expectation, you will get to where you want to be.

Another way to use your imagination is to imagine what failure feels like. Imagine what the consequences will be when you fail. Imagine what the faces of your friends and family will look like when they hear that you have failed. Imagine the pain from the embarrassment you would be facing if that happened and feel every inch of it.

Application: When you embark on a huge and stressful event, use your imagination to imagine your success as well as the pain of failing.

Step 3: Controlling Your Emotions

When your body is going through great stress, a surge in the body's main stress hormones (cortisol, adrenaline, and norepinephrine) will give you a boost of focus and energy. However, if the stress hormones stay at a high surge for a long time, switching to relaxation mode becomes difficult. You will then be faced with sleeping troubles, motivation tumbles, and problems in your immune system.

Breath Control Exercises

Controlling your breath is not limited to controlling arousal; it can also be used to change your state of mind when you are deeply stressed. Navy SEALS and athletes use this technique to control their breath to prepare for a mission or event.

Breath control exercises entail psyching yourself mentally and physically by using deep diaphragmatic breathing, powerful visualization, forced exhalations, and powerful affirmations.

Deep Diaphragmatic Breathing

When you breathe, it happens consciously and unconsciously. Unconscious breathing is referred to as "chest breathing"; it requires energy as it is labor intensive. Chest breathing will lower your energy storage and increase your anxiety.

When you are faced with a difficult mission and are feeling stressed, use the deep diaphragmatic breathing pattern.

You can use this pattern by disciplining yourself with "box breathing". This should be done in a quiet environment.

To use "box breathing", you should inhale and count to 5, hold your breath and count to 5, then exhale and again count to 5. You can do it again or count to 4 if getting to 5 is a little difficult. Now, in four smooth counts, exhale the air that you inhaled, through the nose.

Simple, right? This is closely related to yoga as yogis have been doing this for a very long time now. This method has proven to always be effective and is therefore extremely helpful.

What happens to your brain affects your body, and the other way around too, so use this simple breathing exercise to control your emotions by switching your stress hormones off and preparing the body for relaxation mode.

Let's look at the advantages of using deep diaphragmatic box breathing:

- Controls arousal response.
- Reduces performance anxiety.
- Increases brain performance.
- Increases focus and attention.

Relaxation Breath

This method can be used when in action. Since it is impossible to hold your breath when you are on a mission, using the relaxation breathing technique can help you instead.

To do this, you can drop the part where you hold your breath and just inhale, count to 5 starting from your diaphragm and fill up the middle of your chest as if you are gulping in air, then immediately start exhaling. You can repeat this process again.

This relaxation technique is important as it helps you control your arousal response in order to remain present, in control, and focused. If you keep practicing it, it will eventually become part of you and will become a natural breathing state that provides you with both physical and mental benefits.

Application: If you are already into meditation, this will be of great help. So, the next time you are stressed, take a break with deep breaths before continuing the rest of your day.

Step 4: Mental Stability

As humans, we are all emotional creatures that can easily be affected by things around us or comments about us. In this type of situation, your emotion is at work, and this is where your mental stability comes in.

Just like any other mental skill, your mental stability can be trained to strengthen your general mental health. For this to happen, observe your reaction towards a negative comment, thoughts or events, and keep a tab on how you allow those external factors to get to you and ruin your day.

It is always difficult to keep your cool especially when the closest people to you are driving you nuts. You start getting upset because you feel like they should be the least people offending you.

It isn't bad to expect happiness from your loved ones, so it is totally normal to be upset when they hurt you. However, remember that every time you are upset, it is your fault because you set expectations for them.

The truth is, people are so engrossed in things and don't always think of what they say to you, as well as the consequences of their words. They might not even know their words hurt, so they haven't upset you intentionally. Everyone strives to behave in the best way possible, but our imperfection always sells us out - at one point, we make mistakes. Some people might realize their mistakes while others won't but whatever the case may be, you shouldn't hold grudges or let it get to you.

Their actions towards you might be due to what they are going through - maybe they are having issues at school or work. Always give people around you the benefit of the doubt so that you can make peace with yourself. Show empathy and always put yourself in their shoes. At the end of the day, most of these things wouldn't even matter because you will always forgive yourself for feeling hurt, so why not immediately forgive others and move on?

In order to have that mental stability, you need to stop blaming people around you and instead own up and take full responsibility for expecting too much from people. If someone does not meet your expectations, drop those expectations, and if someone does better than you expected, be appreciative. However, no one owes it to you to behave nicely, so whatever happens, embrace it and move on.

This can also be applied to life. Life owes us nothing when it is good, so be thankful, and when it is bad, don't get sucked in and remain where you are, and dust the negativity off and move on. Use this opportunity to train your mind to be at peace with whatever comes.

Several things can be linked to your mood change, but the origin remains the same. Whatever it may be, identify the cause, modify your reaction, and look at the positive side.

Step 5: Set Goals Aligned with Your Purpose

A lot of people think that you need to work hard to succeed. Undoubtedly, success requires hard work, but you should also know that succeeding doesn't require you to suffer and go through lots of struggle. Succeeding can be done effortlessly, without having to stress yourself too much. So, in a way, you can have fun while succeeding.

A great way to succeed without having to go through unnecessary suffering or working harder than you should is to choose the right goal for you. When your goals are aligned with your purpose, working hard will become fun and you will steadily and easily achieve success.

The goals you set for yourself need to relate to your ethos or should be able to define your purpose in life. Many times, people set goals that don't have a connection to their ethos and when time passes, they start asking themselves what they are doing.

The goals you set should be able to meet up to the challenges in order to never make quitting an option when the going gets tough.

The above techniques should be practiced daily for you to train and develop your mental strength to make it that of an elite warrior.

Chapter 10:
Anti-Habits Holding You Back from Your True Potential

Breaking off bad habits isn't just about stopping them but also about substituting them with other meaningful things. It is always easy to separate the bad from the good, but since you know it is bad, why do you keep doing it? Everyone has the tendency to develop a bad habit but the ability to control it is what differentiate you from others.

Some bad habits are minor, like constantly leaving all your dirty dishes on the table or leaving your clothes on the sofa, while some habits can be worse like being addicted to watching porn, drinking excessive alcohol, and smoking which can affect your health in the long run.

If you feel that you have a habit that is controlling you - this is bad, and you should try to break it and set yourself free. Fighting bad habits is always difficult when you don't have a replacement for it. When you try stopping the habit and become idle, you might just fall back to that bad habit.

It is difficult to break a bad habit is because it has been rooted in your mind due to the constant repetition of the act, especially when it comes to a pleasurable act. The pleasure that it comes with will only get the brain fired up and this will continue even when you stop the habit, as you will now be left struggling with cravings for it. Your ability to control your emotions will determine whether you move past the habit or go back to it.

How Did You Develop Bad Habits?

In order to break free from bad habits, you should know how it became a habit. Habits are a pattern of behavior that started as something insignificant, but when you consciously or unconsciously repeat this behavior, it turns into a habit.

Breaking free from the patterns of this behavior will help you break free from the habits too. Normally, there is a trigger to every pattern, and this trigger can be emotional, environmental, or situational. The emotional trigger is attached to being addicted to drinking and smoking, while an environmental or situational trigger is when you see the dishwasher and a bunch of dirty plates but still decide to leave it for a later time as you still have one clean dish.

This autopilot behavior can be practical to you. When it triggers, it keeps you from re-inventing the normal routine of your daily lives and allows you to make infinite numbers of decisions daily, as well as provides you with enough brain-space to think about other things.

However, the disadvantage of the routine pattern is that it creates more trouble than good.

Easy Steps to Break A Bad Habit

The key to breaking bad habits is becoming aware and identifying them without any form of judgment. Once you have this covered, the next thing to do is to follow the steps to help you break free from it. The reason why you need to become fully aware of this is that when you eventually stop the habit and there is a trigger in your brain that wants you to go back to it, you will be fully aware and know it isn't good for you - just like a reminder.

So, if you have bad habits that you want to break free from, here are some steps to help you get started:

Identify the Triggers

Having so many plates in the kitchen is enough trigger to make you pile up dirty plates because you are made to think that you have not exhausted all the plates in your kitchen yet. Also, the sight of the refrigerator may be a reminder of the fact that there is alcohol in the fridge, ready for you to take. Identifying these triggers means that there is a way for you to push back and not allow the trigger to get a hold of you.

A lot of people are faced with the difficulty of identifying their triggers and when this happens, you can work it out by going backward. For example, if you see your fridge and are really craving a drink, you should slow down and use the responsiveness to this behavior as a signal to ask yourself why you are acting in an uncontrollable manner or what is emotionally wrong with you - that is the trigger you have identified.

Deal with The Triggers

Since you have identified the triggers, the next thing to do is to break loose from that pattern. Here, you should deliberately reduce the number of plates you have in your kitchen or if it is a beer addiction, you should try to reduce the number of beers in your fridge.

Instead of responding to the danger of the triggers, you can do other deliberate things in order to get your mind off the habit, such as engaging in deep breathing to relax your mind when the trigger sets in.

Change the Larger Pattern

Here, the context surrounding your habit-pattern will be explored. For example, you leave your dishes dirty because you still have some clean ones that you can use, or you drink a lot of beer after work because you believe it makes you feel more relaxed. So, you need to start by cleaning up your dirty dishes because you will still have to be the one to do them, and it will ultimately be unavoidable.

When you look at it and change your pattern, you make it easy to tackle the habit and practice putting your willpower in place.

Use Prompts

Using prompts is like a reminder to help you break the pattern by making use of your positive triggers. This will alert you and help you stay on track. Instead of leaving them on the dining table or wherever you used them, try placing your dirty plates on the sink where you can see them, or you even can set a reminder on your phone to alert you when to clean them.

Stop Doing Them

This is obvious. If you want to end a bad habit and swap it with something more meaningful and productive, then it is only right to stop the bad habit. If the habit is not helping you in any way, why are you still doing it?

Develop A Substitute Plan

As mentioned earlier, breaking loose from bad habits isn't all about stopping as it also involves substituting the habit with something else.

How do you stop drinking when you are with friends that drink? Or, how can you manage not to drink at a party where everyone is drinking? You can substitute your beer drinking habit and grab a mocktail instead and hang out with people that you can make conversation with instead of giving in to the beer trigger.

If you want to avoid getting tempted to smoke, you can substitute it with eating your favorite snack or if you are addicted to porn, you can help yourself by getting a book to read when you feel bored or even going out with friends in order to take your mind off it.

This trigger will always present itself and it can kick in at any time but if you are ready to get rid of your bad habit, you need to set a new direction for yourself. Instead of indulging in a habit that will only bring you pain and regret, you can do other fun stuff like exercise, read a book, or even meditate.

Attach A Bigger Purpose Behind Your Change

People decide that they want to cut off a habit because it is believed to be a bad habit and the right thing to do is to get rid of it. Instead of saying it is the right thing to do, why not say it is an absolute must to get rid of it? This will show your readiness and help keep the triggers at bay.

Now, you can only see the bigger purpose if you can answer the following questions - why do you want to get rid of the habit? Is it really a bad habit? Has it been affecting your progress? Will your life be better off without it?

Once you can answer these questions and come to the realization that the habit is bad and that you need to get rid of it, it's time to attach it to a bigger purpose.

Perhaps drinking too many beers is beginning to affect your health and it's showing, or you are addicted to watching porn and it's affecting your relationship and your mental health; so, why not make a huge difference by using that energy for a bigger purpose?

You can put this energy towards a skill you have always wanted to acquire but haven't found the time to, or even a side business you've always wanted to run. The bad habit does not serve a bigger purpose, so why not add more fuel to your change and focus on bigger things?

Get Support

When it proves difficult to curtail the habit or to stay in control, you can seek support from a friend. Get support from someone you can easily call, talk to, or get motivation from when the cravings kick in. A close friend can be very helpful, especially one that doesn't have the bad habits that you are trying to push aside.

You can hang out with your buddy and grab a cup of coffee instead of drinking beer. Spend time together, talk, and express how you feel, as this will help you.

However, if you have really done your best and still can't overcome the habit, it is time to seek professional help. This can be a doctor that will prescribe the right medication for you because the habit has become chronic and risks being a disorder.

Another way to go about this is to see a therapist that will not only help you work on the source and trigger of your habits but will also give you the necessary support that you need.

All bad habits are not the same or created equally but they all have an all-encompassing goal which is to give you a setback. Take charge of your life, be more proactive, and be deliberate in everything you do.

Stay Consistent

When you are looking at leaving those bad habits behind you for good, consistency is key. It took time for the bad habit to root and plant itself in your brain, so it will take time for it to be uprooted and replaced with another habit.

The strategy to go with is consistency. You must stay consistent with the new habit and engage with it more. The more you engage with it, the more your brain registers and adapts to it. Your brain will get wired around it and it will become easier to trigger the new habit than the bad one.

If you want to stop drinking beer, substitute it with another drink and as you start to drink it often, your brain will register it due to consistency.

Chapter 11:
Why Losers Never Get Better

Why do you need to win? Why do people lose? How do you win? What are the differences between a winner and a loser?

These are essential questions that you need to know the answer to. By nature, humans are very competitive, with an exaggerated sense of self-importance. We always want to prove we are just a little better than others or even than our own selves. We can't help ourselves from competing; in fact, in this world, we compete for almost everything. That is the dividing line between "winners" and "losers".

Why Do You Need to Win?

When you have a goal and want to achieve it, it will naturally lead to competition. At some point, your greatest competitor is yourself and for you to be victorious, you must first conquer the old you. Some goals are simple, and due to the surrounding circumstances, they are easy to achieve. Other goals may be extremely difficult, and to achieve them, you will need a lot of hard work, dedication, and a powerful mental state to attain victory and be successful.

Everyone needs to be a winner at some point to prove to themselves and their surroundings that they don't just exist but are truly alive.

Then Why Do People Lose?

Because they fail to achieve the desired outcome of their initial goal and fail to try again and again.

"I've missed more than 9000 shots in my career. I've lost almost 300 games. 26 times, I've been trusted to take the game winning shot and missed. I've failed over and repeatedly in my life. And that is why I succeed". – Michael Jordan

How Do You Win?

Just like the quote above, failing doesn't mean that you have lost. Losing is when you stop trying to improve on what you did wrong. When you are determined to work on your set goal, take solid action until you achieve the result that you aimed for. The continuous actions that you have taken express your attitude towards success.

What Are the Differences Between A Winner and A Loser?

There has never been a real competition between a winner and a loser. At times, it may seem like people are just destined to succeed and win at every turn and progress unhindered, while others stagnate and can't accomplish anything. The dividing line between these two people is down to their attitudes and habits.

Most people with success stories usually have a long history of failures, but that doesn't mean they are losers. Yes! They have failed several times, but with the right attitude, mindset, habits, and actions, they persist until they achieve success.

The mindset of every individual can influence and determine if they are a winner or a loser. Let's look at some of the differences between the winner and the loser's mindset and understand what separates them.

Winners

- Winners will admit their mistakes, learn from them and try to improve.
- When there is a challenge, winners focus on the solutions.
- Winners will work hard whether someone is watching or not, as they are self-motivated.
- Winners set goals.
- Winners are consistent; they understand that the best way to achieve the desired successful outcome is consistency.
- Winners change strategies and explore other options when the initial plan is not working.
- Winners understand that when they fail, it is also a learning process, and it is treated as a learning experience on the road to success.
- Winners understand the influence of the people that surround them, so they surround themselves with people who can bring the best out of them.
- Winners are people who give back.
- Winners don't dwell in their comfort zone; they constantly seek to expand their boundaries.
- Winners have the mindset of "I must do something".
- Winners will put forth the maximum amount of effort when they take on any task.

Losers

- Losers will blame others for their mistakes and make excuses.
- Losers focus on problems.
- Losers will avoid work; they will only do what's needed for them to get by unless there's someone keeping an eye on them.
- Losers will expect to see and achieve results they desire and want to see the outcome overnight.
- Losers are afraid of setting goals.
- Losers keep repeating the same thing they did that didn't work repeatedly, expecting a different result.
- Losers are easily overwhelmed and tend to give up immediately as they are met with rejection or any form of failure.
- Losers will usually surround themselves with like-minded losers.
- Losers stay within the boundaries of their comfort zone.
- Losers have the philosophy of taking more and giving less or even giving nothing at all.
- Losers will say, "Something must be done"
- Losers will put in the least amount of effort required to meet the minimum criteria on a task.

7 Qualities That Define A Winner

1. Only Set Clearly Defined Goals

If you want to achieve reasonable results in anything you do, you first need to clearly define your goals. Someone without clearly defined goals is like a sailor without a navigating compass. When you set definite goals, it's like a compass that guides you towards a certain direction.

In order to win, you must be SMART in setting your goals. The SMART goal means:

Specific: you have a target area you want to work on.

Measurable: your goals are quantifiable, measurable, or can be gauged or viewed to take a certain dimension.

Assignable: your goals should be assignable, and you should be able to decide the place of a certain thing in the bigger picture where something belongs in a general scheme and who will do the task

Realistic: make sure that your goals are achievable and doable. Imagine setting a goal of counting the hairs on your head, which is totally unrealistic. Set goals that can be done within a period.

Time-bound: when your goals have a timeframe, it will unconsciously trigger the mental alarm that will drive you to achieve your goals within that time limit. Long goals without a time limit might lead to developing the habit of procrastination.

This acronym will enable you to turn your desired goals into normal habits and achieve success.

2. Self-Projection

What is self-projection? It simply means that you have a vivid and clear picture of your goals and what you really want to achieve.

Self-projection is basically knowing what your end goal should look like and keeping it in mind. But to winners, self-projection is much more than just knowing your end goal. It requires life and mental animation, so you can imagine a movie and play the scenes in your head, where you are the lead role in achieving that goal.

For example, if you want to climb a mountain, you can visualize the mountain climb you are planning, and you can see yourself climbing, sweating, overcoming challenges, and conquering the tasks nature has set for you. Having a solid and vivid view of your goals be a form of mental affirmation and will increase excitement.

3. Play to Win and Stay Positive

Losers are people who always worry. Instead of playing to win, they play not to lose. A loser will say "what if I'm not doing it right" while a winner will say "I believe I am doing it right". They go in with a positive mental attitude as well as the confidence to get it right.

When you find yourself using "What ifs", like "What if I don't hit the target when I shoot?" "What if I fail at my task?", "What if the boss hates me?", you are displaying the attitude of a loser.

Nothing good comes out of the excessive fear of losing; you will only worry yourself and become stressed and ultimately end up achieving nothing. Also, you will likely miss out on opportunities, fail at your tasks, or fail to accomplish your set goals.

Visualize yourself winning and see yourself achieving your goals. Replace all the "what ifs" with positive thoughts and an optimistic mindset.

4. Be Active and Not Passive (Self-Determination)

When you are taking on any task, be actively involved and own that project, and at that moment, make it your set goal. Visualize yourself successfully completing the project. Act passively, and don't do it just because your boss wants you to.

Winning and losing are all within your control, and if you take charge, you are directly controlling and directing the flow of success towards you. It means you have taken matters into your own hands and have not left it to fate because you are a self-determined person.

As a self-determined person, you influence things to work and happen according to your tactics, and you make sure nothing keeps you from achieving your goals. Winners change strategies and explore other options, and when their initial plan is not working, they always have a plan B.

When you are passive and have the mindset of a loser, you naturally "let things occur" while you just watch.

5. Self–Awareness

Winning or being a winner does not mean that you should be perfect, and it does not mean that you should use any means necessary to succeed without caring about the consequences.

It should be about understanding that you are not perfect and identifying your weaknesses to make plans to fix them. One quality of a winner is knowing the right thing at the right time. Also, to succeed, you don't have to do everything by yourself. Learn when to delegate tasks and outsource those that require a professional.

Focus on what you are good that and let others who are better than you at other aspects handle those. That way, you get things done quicker and you still win. It is all about knowing and understanding yourself.

Once you are self-aware, you can easily empathize with others. If you can feel and understand what those around you feel, you will have a broader understanding and know when to act and when not to.

When you understand yourself, you can understand others better as well; self-awareness can make you more adaptable to sudden changes, your adaptability will help you adjust on-the-go, and the chances that your set goals crash and fail due to sudden changes will be very low, so you will always be on track to succeed.

6. Self-Discipline

Most people would rather take the easy way out because no one really likes the fact that success requires a lot of work. Since we are in the real world, there are no hacks, shortcuts, or cheat codes.

To be successful, you must start from the very beginning, from the setting of goals to the planning and execution phases. To achieve all those, you need to build and maintain the habits that will lead you to your goals. One of these habits is self-discipline, where you set goals and see them through to the end, no matter what.

If you are a procrastinator, one of the ways to counter it is to incorporate self-discipline in your routine to keep you going.

7. Live in The Present

If you dwell in the past, your future will be foggy because you are compromising your present and have forgotten the value of time.

Once the past is gone, leave it in the past because you have the present where you can try repeatedly. The past should be viewed as a reference book that you learn from; you can consult it and learn from your past mistakes, but don't remain and wallow in the past.

All winners aim for the future by setting up SMART goals and acting upon them. Their projections cover years into the future, and they imagine how secure it will be. It will do you no good to set future goals and daydream all day about how the future will turn out or what it could hold and counting your future successes without acting. What you need today is the present because without it, you will have a compromised future with no success.

Winners take immediate action and work with the present, consult with the past, and project for the future. They plan time efficiently and have enough to spend with their family and loved ones.

5 Habits to Give Up If You Want to Be Successful

Some people have given up on pursuing their aspirations because they feel that their efforts will be in vain. They believe that it is their fault for not being successful in all their endeavors, they don't consider themselves intelligent, and therefore, their growth will be determined by fate.

What you should know and understand is that being successful cannot be hindered because you are not the most talented or brilliant; however, bad habits can do so. The following are 5 toxic habits that you quickly need to get rid of if you want to be successful.

Habit 1: Leave Your Comfort Zone

When you feel things are stagnated and you are just living your life on a repeat, it is time to explore new grounds, expand your horizon, and make new experiences. Whatever you do, don't just remain where you were; if you must crawl, do so and leave your comfort zone.

If you are performing the same job daily, reliving the same morning habits and ending up the night the same way, as well as have the same set of friends and same experiences, it is time to stop living the same month or year over and over, because you can't keep using the same strategy and expect different results.

You need to mix up daily routine, friends, and habits by changing your environment, creating new challenges, and finding new opportunities. Just leave your comfort zone as often as you can and experience new things, as variety is often said to be the spice of life.

Try thinking differently; take up a new hobby, do a road trip, sign up to take a class, or even teach one. Just challenge yourself, your body and your mind.

Habit 2: Pressure of People's Expectations of You

When you worry too much about people's opinion of you, you will have a tough time succeeding at many things. Your family, co-workers, boss, and boyfriend/girlfriend are all different individuals and will never know exactly how it feels to be you.

Allowing the expectations of others to weigh you down will only place you in a position where all you do is satisfy their expectations of you. If you fail to meet up to their expectations, it might lead to them having bad opinion of you, as well as ruining your connections and important relationships with them.

You need to stop letting the opinions and the expectations of others dictate who you are. Learn how to set your own expectations and they will naturally be forced to view you as an individual with a will and a mind of his own. You must make them realize that you can be trusted to determine success in your own way.

Habit 3: Quit Being Around the Same People

Take a pen and paper and write down the names of the people who surround you, then review them one after the other and ask yourself the following questions:

Do they add value to you and help you or do they pull you down and hurt you?

Do they make you a better person by challenging you to become better or Do they help you take care of/settle tough situations?

Do you gain new experiences, learn from them, and get inspired by them?

If you mostly answered no, it's time to start being around a new set of people who can positively impact your life, inspire you, challenge you, and give you knew experiences. Be around people who can show you how to set goals and plan.

If your friends are not helping you, they are hurting you. So, how do you find new like-minded people who can challenge you, inspire you, and add value to your life?

Attend a party that fits your preference as you will meet people that like the same things as you. Attend a seminar about a topic that interests you and you will meet like-minded people at the venue.

Habit 4: Quit Procrastinating

Unlike other bad habits, procrastination steals your time and paralyzes your future without you even being aware of it.

When you procrastinate, you find it difficult to set goals and take the first step, and you look for excuses to find a way to undertake your tasks later.

People who procrastinate always forget that time will never wait for anyone, yet with limited time, they'd rather accomplish an unimportant task than face what they set out to. For example, when you are supposed to file a report or audit an account for your company, you use that time to play video games or use social media.

People who are successful always make the most of the limited time that is available to them because they are focused and know how to prioritize and set goals. These kinds of people will only engage in habits that will keep them in a state of continuous growth and increased productivity.

Habit 5: Quit Dwelling on Past Failures

There can hardly be any success story with tasting the sour taste of failure. The ability to rise above failure or disappointment is what defines you as a fighter who deserves to be successful.

When you fail or make mistakes, it is fine to blame yourself a little; however, when you continuously sink into self-blame and self-pity, it does you more harm than good. So, instead of beating yourself up and being a sore loser, you should consider it an opportunity to learn on your journey to success.

Don't destroy yourself for failing; direct that anger towards the failure instead and destroy it. Review your old decisions to find out where you went wrong, why you failed, and what you can do to get a different outcome.

Find a reason to always do it again, change your strategy, adopt a new plan, be flexible, and remain focused and determined that you will get it right if you try it one last time.

Chapter 12:
Forge an Unrelentless Mind and Never Stay Down

Success requires hard work, and the journey to being successful is filled with tough challenges. So, one of the most important tools you will need to succeed is "mental toughness".

When you are confronted with challenges, do you do what it takes to persist and overcome those challenges? Do you do whatever you can to never quit and try one more time every time you fail? When you put determination, willpower, endurance, resilience, and strength all together, in psychology, this is called "mental toughness", and this is what you need to fight your way and struggle through all obstacles to succeed.

When the term mental toughness is mentioned, I would like you to picture athletes who persevere through exhaustion, endure injury, and push themselves to the limit to win - that strength they display is called mental toughness. Another example is a combatant soldier who will grit and endure the fatigue and tired muscles yet will still carry the weight of a wounded comrade on his back to seek medical attention from the battlefield.

Mental toughness has created many superstar gold-winning athletes as well as hero soldiers. The question now is - how do you build mental toughness? How can your tough mental attitude fit into all aspects of your life and help you be successful?

Understanding the Essential Components of Mental Toughness

Mental toughness doesn't just help make great athletes, as many other successful people all over the world have used mental toughness, one way or the other. Before you start building and developing these qualities, you should first know what makes mentally strong people different from others.

Although it might have originated from sports and the military, defining the ability to endure, persevere, remain confident, and stay strong and competitive, it is also now widely used in different fields, and people can now build and develop these qualities to handle difficulties in life.

It helps people in different circumstances effectively deal with changing situations, challenges, pressure, and even factors that might cause stress.

There are 4 key components to these personality qualities:

Control: Puts you in charge and keeps you from losing control to others. You are the controller of every action you take, including your emotions. Your ability to handle, manage and respond to situations is one of your main abilities. You have a firm belief that your destiny and life are fully under your control.

- Challenge: Challenges are viewed as opportunities rather than obstacles.
- Commitment: The ability to undertake tasks until the very end.
- Confidence: Having an unshakable self-belief in your capabilities and ability to be successful.

Qualities of mental toughness can be acquired, trained and developed to fit into various areas of your life and enable you to become successful. To become a mentally tough person, it requires training and consistency.

Positive Self-Talk

SEALs and Athletes all utilize positive talks, especially before, during, and after a mission. The words that you say need to be said in a positive light. It has been estimated that in a minute, you say about 300 – 1000 words to yourself. This is because your brain is a complex part of your body that is always running, and it keeps track of everything you say or do.

When it comes to world-renowned athletes, they believe there is nothing negative in their ways and all they must do is give it their absolute best.

What about SEALs - what method do they employ? Well, they use similar methods; however, theirs are way scarier and can even be considered terrifying.

Imagine yourself underwater with your breathing gear, and without expecting it, your gear is snatched from your mouth, and the oxygen lines are tied into a knot, leaving you to figure out what to do.

The first thing your brain will do is send an alarm, telling you that "you are going to choke to death." However, what you need to do is stay calm while you are underwater and follow the procedure to untie the knot and breathe again.

Your brain starts screaming, "YOU ARE GOING TO DIE." But you must keep cool, stay underwater, and follow the procedure to get your gear working so you can breathe again.

The dangerous part of this drill is panic. For SEALs, panicking is not allowed, so even when they are not able to breathe, they must maintain a clear and calm head.

How can you relate to this and apply it in other fields of your life? I'm sure you have figured it out by now.

The idea is that no matter the obstacle you are facing, if you have a big project or a complex presentation, you are not allowed to panic. Stay calm and think positive. Remember that you are durable and can outlast any problem, so you just must think.

A pessimist (a loser) will immediately hit the panic button, believing bad situations will last for a very long time or even forever and will say: "There is no way that I can ever get this done." Or, "I am bad at handling this type of thing, I can't do it, and it is not my fault".

An optimist (a winner) will view the obstacles or setbacks in a different way because they have a strong belief that bad things are just temporary and will say: "That sort of thing occasionally happens, but it's no big deal." Or "I know it is not my fault, I am usually good at handling such things, but today was just not my day."

Building mental toughness always requires you to talk positively to yourself and to always remain optimistic.

Build an Unshakable Belief in Your Ability to Achieve Your Goals

When it comes to success, one thing most gold-winning athletes have in common is an "unshakable self-belief".

People with a tough mental attitude don't just think they might win or succeed; they strongly believe that they will. A warrior will never go out thinking that he might succeed; he has the mindset that he will succeed and return to his family and loved ones. When you apply these concepts to other fields of your life, you will get positive results.

Whether you are planning to run a marathon race, shed some weight, quit a bad habit, or do better on a pending task, believe in yourself and tell yourself that you can do it. Be self-encouraging, avoid any form of negative talks and self-doubt, stay positive, and be prepared to carry out what you set your mind to all the way to the end.

Practice Visualization

Close your eyes, relax your mind, and picture a big challenge. Now, imagine yourself as you walk through the challenges step by step. This is a strategy that even the best Olympians and SEALs use. They play it in their mind and watch themselves do it repeatedly.

Athletes are trained daily to develop their imagery skills. They use this method of imagery to get themselves prepared to achieve what they want from their training session. They perfect different skills with imagination, make technical corrections before the actual training commences, and are even able to visualize themselves winning the competition and achieving their goals.

SEALs are also trained and thought to do the same thing; they undergo mental rehearsals where they are taught the techniques to visualize themselves succeeding in a given task, and they are required to go through the steps through visualization.

When SEALs have an important mission, they spend hours every day visualizing any possible error or problem they might encounter during the mission and counter it by creating a visual solution. They go over many scenarios and different possibilities and fix them. They visualize things like a wrong drop zone, a sudden appearance of enemy troops and other problems and emergencies.

How Do You Apply This Strategy?

You need to open your mind, close your eyes and visualize the task that you have before you. Don't just start a fantasy and fantasize that everything is alright and perfect and make yourself feel good about it. This will kill your drive and motivation.

Positive fantasy can cause poor performances and fewer achievements, and the reason is that people can get carried away by the fantasy of visualizing a perfect goal, and at the end of the day, they don't have enough energy to physically pursue their desired goal.

Visualization is aimed to enable you to see the possible problems that you might face and visualize how to solve them.

Now that you are at the stage of visualizing how your big day will be like; you can walk through it step by step to see how you will handle any possible problem.

Use Simulations

The visualization technique is awesome; you can practice it as many times as you want, and you can do it anywhere you are comfortable. However, at the end of it all, you need to also practice hard because practicing is the physical simulation of the real deal.

All medal-winning athletes around the world make use of simulation training extensively. They practice over and over to the point where they breakdown from physical exhaustion and fatigue. They practice as if they were already at the competition, and even wear what they would the day of the actual competition, as well as undergo routines and preparations that they would on the main day.

How Do You Apply This Strategy?

If you have been preparing for a presentation that requires you to stand in front of a large crowd, how are you going to deal with the fear and anxiety that comes with it?

If you are an introvert, or you are just not used to making presentations in front of a crowd, you can use simulation as well. Start by practicing in front of your mirror, then in front of small groups. You can also make use of a supportive group and rehearse in front of them. From there, you can evaluate yourself and find out where you are lacking and how to fix this.

SEALs and athletes are the best at doing their jobs, and we can use the same methods as them to succeed and get results through preparation and hard work.

Conclusion

This journey has been amazing, and we hope that by now, you've been able to gather more than just a few things about exploring the chances that are within you to be whoever you want to be. The mind is like the sky, wide enough for you to explore as much as you are willing to, without a barrier. While flying, the possible obstacles that you may encounter are only physical and like a bird, you may either choose to fly above them or go below. Whatever the case may be, it is essential to eliminate every possibility of quitting. Always tell yourself that it is possible.

If a person can go through a thing as severe as the Navy SEAL training, what can't you do? It's all in your mind, and the most significant barriers are those you have created yourself. What makes you succeed at a task that others have failed is your perspective; if you choose to see the positive side of everything, you will excel even beyond your imagination. It is important to note that everything you are is as a result of your interaction with the world. If you seem to be failing where others are excelling, it is not because failure is part of your DNA, but because you have not acquired the necessary skills to excel. You came to the world as a blank slate, so make conscious efforts to infuse positive things into yourself all the time.

Make sure that with every day that passes, you have taken steps to be better than the previous day. Life is a continuous process of self-development, so never stop working on yourself until the day you die. At the end of it all, everyone dies, but not everyone gets the chance to live, so before you die, make sure you have lived.

If you find this book helpful in anyway a review to support my endeavors is much appreciated.